THIS WORLD
IS NOT
MY HOME

REFLECTIONS FOR PILGRIMS ON THE WAY

MARK G. JOHNSTON

THE BANNER OF TRUTH TRUST

THE BANNER OF TRUTH TRUST

Head Office	*North America Office*
3 Murrayfield Road	PO Box 621
Edinburgh, EH12 6EL	Carlisle, PA 17013
UK	USA

banneroftruth.org

© Mark G. Johnston 2021
First published 2021

*

ISBN
Print: 978 1 80040 151 8
Epub: 978 1 80040 152 5
Kindle: 978 1 80040 153 2

*

Typeset in 11/14 Adobe Garamond Pro at
The Banner of Truth Trust, Edinburgh

Printed in the USA by
Versa Press Inc.,
East Peoria, IL

THIS WORLD IS NOT MY HOME

For

Steven and Gail

fellow travellers and great encouragers

Contents

Preface

Every book has a story in the sense of a plot line, or narrative; but it also has some kind of back-story, a history explaining why it was written. So it is with this book. It had a previous existence in a different form, as part of a collection of articles. It was only after the suggestion of some friends that I decided to select 30 of them for a wider readership.

In their original form, they appeared in a monthly column on *Place for Truth*, an online resource of the *Alliance of Confessing Evangelicals*—a coalition of pastors, scholars, and churchmen who hold the historic creeds and confessions of the Reformed faith and who proclaim biblical doctrine in order to foster a Reformed awakening in today's church.

The title of the column is *Resident Aliens*. This too is significant in terms of how this book came into being and for the underlying plot line holding it together. I chose the title while I was living in America and pastoring a church there and had become used to the designation 'resident alien' to define my immigration status in that country. I smiled every time I thought about it, because it actually echoes the Bible's designation for the spiritual residency status we have as Christians in this world. Although in this life our 'home' is planet earth, it is only as temporary residents. We actually and ultimately belong somewhere else. Our citizenship is in heaven.

Even though the articles that have appeared in my column over the years range far and wide in terms of their scope, they are all connected by the underlying thought, in the words of Albert E. Brumley's old song, often sung by African American congregrations, that:

This world is not my home;
  I'm just a passing through;
My treasures are laid up,
  Somewhere beyond the blue.

Hence the title for this book and so too its subtitle: *Reflections for pilgrims on the Way.*

I am enormously grateful to Robert Brady, Jeff Stivason, Jonathan Master, Karen Ciavolella as well as the board of the *Alliance of Confessing Evangelicals* for the privilege of working with them in a variety of ways for the past ten years and longer. Their work has had and continues to have a far-reaching influence for good as they promote historic and confessional Reformed Christianity in the United States and beyond.

I am also grateful to the Banner of Truth Trust for its willingness to publish this book. It too has served the church both in the United Kingdom and throughout the world with the same desire to promote the Reformed Faith in the spirit of Reformed catholicity that characterised the Reformers as well as their heirs and successors, the Puritans.

Since the heart of what follows will focus on what it means for us as Christians to be pilgrims passing through this fallen world, I thought it fit to dedicate this book to two fellow-pilgrims who have been wonderful travelling companions and true encouragers to me and my family over the many years we have known each other. They are Steven and Gail Curry. Together they have demonstrated again and again that although at times the journey will be tough, it is always suffused with joy from heaven.

MARK G. JOHNSTON
Trinity Church Evangelical Presbyterian
Richhill, Co. Armagh
August 2021

Foreword

It is a privilege for me to provide a Foreword for Mark Johnston's latest book, *This World Is Not My Home*. I have known Mark for twenty-five years and have increasingly prized his friendship, encouragement and counsel.

Over these years I have worked closely with Mark on numerous projects and have always been blessed with his commitment, passion and gospel catholicity. I mention these things to say that within the pages of *This World Is Not My Home* you will find writing that is pastoral, thoughtful, encouraging, challenging, and above all radically God-centred.

The thirty brief but compelling chapters remind us that 'this world is not our home,' that our destiny is a 'city that has foundations, whose designer and builder is God' (Heb. 11:10), and that within those two horizons we are called to live world-engaging, Christ-glorifying lives.

These brief chapters have many strengths, but perhaps their greatest strength is to give the reader a sense of the cosmic drama of Christ's redemption, from its beginnings in the wake of Adam's tragic fall in humanity's first home, the garden of Eden, to its consummation in the new heavens and new earth.

I have no doubt that any Christian who reads this book will be instructed, challenged, encouraged, and compelled to bless God for the 'so great salvation' that he has accomplished in the Lord Jesus Christ and given as a gift of his grace to his believing people. This is an ideal primer for young Christians to give them a cosmic perspective on the believing life, and an engaging reminder to older Christians to live as pilgrims pressing onwards and upwards to our eternal home, where God in his triune glory dwells.

IAN HAMILTON
Inverness

Introduction

LONG before they were ever called 'Christians,' those who embraced the promise of salvation through Jesus Christ were known as 'followers of the Way.' It was the most obvious way to identify and describe them, because their life and destiny were publicly bound to the one who said, 'I am the way, the truth and the life' (John 14:6). In saying this, Jesus was not simply saying he would 'point the way' to life; but for all who are joined to him in saving union, he is all three simultaneously. He embodies the journey that takes us ultimately out of the depths of our lostness to the heights of our everlasting home in heaven.

The saviour is simply picking up on the fact that the Old Testament Scriptures are full of the imagery of life as a journey. One that is travelled not simply with the passing of the years—however many or few they may be—from the cradle to the grave, but one that is also travelled in the sobering light of where it ultimately leads in the world to come.

Moses captures this thought in Psalm 90, which opens with the declaration, 'Lord, you have been our dwelling place in all generations' (Psa. 90:1). He points to God himself as the great constant in every aspect of life in this world for all who believe. Other psalms also pick up this theme by pointing to the exodus when God took his people out of the bondage of Egypt into the freedom of the Promised Land.

Tied in with this, an entire section of the Book of Psalms has been labelled, 'The Songs of Ascent.' These were pilgrim songs, used by Israelites as they travelled up to Jerusalem for the annual feasts and festivals in the Temple. They all focus ultimately on the Lord as their covenant God and saviour, and Zion as the earthly symbol of the hope of heaven. Yet they do so in a way that reflects the struggles and challenges God's people experience along the way; and, even more so, God's never-failing faithfulness to those who trust him.

The entire message of the Bible can rightly be summed up as the journey in which God alone can lead us. It is a journey that takes us from being alienated from God through Adam's disobedience, to being reconciled to him through Christ, and ultimately to the perfect home he is preparing for us in the new heavens and new earth.

It was the Baptist tinker-preacher, John Bunyan, who captured this key thought from the Bible in a most enduring way. During his twelve-year imprisonment for simply preaching the gospel, he penned his most famous work, *Pilgrim's Progress*. With captivating style and rich theological insight he takes his readers through the journey that led Christian out of the City of Destruction, through the many twists and turns of his experience in the life of faith, to his arrival in the Celestial City—heaven. The fact this 340-year-old volume still ranks among the top best-selling books of all time speaks for itself in terms of its ability to convey rich biblical truth to all kinds of people in all kinds of circumstances. It helps us understand what it really means 'to be a pilgrim.'

It is for these reasons that I have selected the articles that are included in this volume. My aim is very much to help readers who are already Christians but are perhaps struggling with the unusual and often unexpected twists and turns of the life of faith. As the apostle Peter says, far from being something strange, suffering is in fact normal Christian experience (1 Pet. 4:12).

I would love to think there might be others who delve into these pages who have not yet come to believe in the Christ of the Bible, but nevertheless are curious as to what it means to become a Christian. If this happens to be you, then I do hope this book will give you answers; and that these answers assure you that, even though Jesus calls us to 'take up the cross' to follow after him, the joys and blessings of the new life he gives are more than worth its cost.

What follows has been divided into five sections. They are of differing lengths, but are intended to flow into each other to give a sense of how the theme of the Christian life as a spiritual journey is presented from a variety of angles in the Bible.

The first section seeks to summarise the history of redemption. That is, the grand narrative of all that God has planned, promised, and done to redeem and rescue a people for himself. From the perfection of Eden when creation was complete, through Adam's great rebellion, on to God's promise to send a saviour and how this was fulfilled in Christ, and ultimately to the restoration that will come when he returns. If we are Christians, this is our story. Everything we read in Scripture from Genesis to Revelation relates to us. We can only understand ourselves truly when we see our place first with fallen humanity in Adam, and then—through Jesus Christ—in the redeemed humanity destined for heaven.

Section Two is devoted entirely to Jesus Christ. It is, as Sinclair Ferguson has said, only as we begin to understand him that we begin to understand ourselves, if we are believers. He is not only the one who saves us, he is the template for the new life we receive and begin to work out as God's new humanity.

The third section takes us into the realm of the church of Jesus Christ, what it means and why it matters that we as Christians are part of it. For many in this twenty-first century world, the Christian life can feel unnecessarily lonely. The reason for this is because many have lost sight of the fact that to be a Christian means being part of God's redeemed community—the church as the body of Christ. Appreciating what this means is guaranteed to bring a whole new dimension into how we understand the new life to which he has called us and how we face the journey that lies before us.

It may surprise some readers that the fourth section, which deals more narrowly with the Christian life in terms of what it means for us as individuals, is the shortest section. In part this is deliberate. Our generation has exalted individual identity above the shared identity found in community. Perhaps not surprisingly, our generation has also experienced more confusion and struggle in our personal lives—even as Christians—because we have tried to 'go it alone.'

The final section picks up on another vital, but often neglected theme for pilgrims on the way. It is the theme of joy. The spirit in which we travel is that of the joy of heaven which has come down to earth. Too much professed Christianity founders along the way because it is joyless. As we begin to appreciate that 'the joy of the Lord is our strength' (Neh. 8:10), it will be our great encouragement to press on towards the goal of heaven that lies at the end of the road and the perfect joy that will be ours in that place for evermore.

SECTION ONE

FROM EDEN TO THE NEW JERUSALEM

For you have not come to what may be touched, a blazing fire and darkness and gloom and a tempest and the sound of a trumpet and a voice whose words made the hearers beg that no further messages be spoken to them. For they could not endure the order that was given, 'If even a beast touches the mountain, it shall be stoned.' Indeed, so terrifying was the sight that Moses said, 'I tremble with fear.' But you have come to Mount Zion and to the city of the living God, the heavenly Jerusalem, and to innumerable angels in festal gathering, and to the assembly of the first-born who are enrolled in heaven, and to God, the judge of all, and to the spirits of the righteous made perfect, and to Jesus, the mediator of a new covenant, and to the sprinkled blood that speaks a better word than the blood of Abel.

Hebrews 12:18-24

I

Aliens and Strangers

THERE is something deep within the human psyche that longs to be 'home'—to be settled in a place where we belong. Yet, for many, this is a frustrated longing. For some it is because, by virtue of their circumstances, they are dislocated from where they want to be. Perhaps because of schooling, or the demands of work, they are always on the move. Or it may be for more tragic reasons: they have been driven from their home and are now refugees in someone else's homeland. For others, even though they may be physically 'at home,' they live with a deep restlessness of soul because the reality of home life never seems to measure up to their ideals and expectations.

It is possible to explore this from a host of angles—as psychologists and sociologists so often do—but for the sake of this opening chapter I want to focus on one angle: the one found in the Bible. There we discover dimensions to our sense of 'rootlessness' that go far deeper than our immediate circumstances of life. The apostle Peter captures this vividly when he addresses his readers as 'aliens and strangers' (1 Pet. 2:11 NIV) as the means of helping them grasp where they really belong as people of faith, and how to live their life on earth in light of it.

In a very broad sense, the roots of this rootlessness run right back to the garden of Eden: the 'home' God gave our first parents, Adam and Eve. Even though, at the end of the process of creation, God saw that all he had made was 'very good' (Gen. 1:31), the goodness of the garden itself had more to it than met the eye. In part this was because it was the location of the tree of life and the tree of the knowledge of good and evil (Gen. 2:9), which would ultimately determine whether or not Adam and Eve would enjoy life to the full. But in an even more profound sense, it was the place where the omnipresent God—whom the heavens cannot contain (1 Kings 8:27)—presenced himself personally and communed with Adam and his wife (Gen. 3:8). It was both 'home' and heaven on earth because God, it seems, habitually met with them there.

The second chapter of Genesis gives us a brief, but tanta-lising glimpse of what that perfect earthly home looked and felt like. And not only was it filled with potential for the 'life to the full' that mankind was intended to enjoy, but as the human race multiplied and human beings fulfilled their God-given mandate to be stewards of the entire world and cosmos, the blessings cradled in the garden would flow to the ends of the universe. Sadly, that potential was not to be realised—at least not within the framework of the original world order.

Adam rebelled against God and brought God's curse, not only upon himself and his spouse, but also upon creation in its entirety (Gen. 3:14-19; Rom. 5:12-14). What did that look like in the immediate aftermath of the fall? Was Eden transformed into some kind of a post-atomic fallout zone? Interestingly, apart from the description of what God's curse and the entrance of death would entail for Adam and the world, the most visible difference is Adam and Eve being expelled from the garden that was meant to be their home and the implication that somewhere in that place there were now two bloodied carcasses of animals sacrificially slaughtered by God to provide a covering for them (Gen. 3:21, 24).

Of course, the primary significance of their expulsion from Eden is not that they have been driven from a residence, but from a relationship. Eden had been their 'home' up until that point, not because of its grandeur, beauty and homeliness, but because God was there to enjoy fellowship with them. Adam and Eve were now aliens and strangers in what had once been their homeland because they had become alienated and estranged from the God who had given it to them.

This double-edged estrangement is very quickly seen to be the essence of the human predicament. For all the beauty and richness of the earth—even under God's curse—it had become a place of 'dis-*ease*' for the children of Adam. Even the very best the world could provide could not satisfy. The words of God to Cain after he had murdered his brother Abel capture the universal experience of humanity from that point onward: 'You will be a homeless wanderer on the earth' (Gen. 4:12 NET). But it is Cain's response that explains why this would be so: 'from your face I shall be hidden' (Gen. 4:14).

As we try to make sense of the here and now in this world, it is here we must begin: the sense of being dislocated from our environment and from our fellow human beings—that is so pervasive—actually has its roots in the fact that, in our natural state, we are all dislocated from God. We'll explore this theme more fully in the following chapters. Thankfully, the Bible does not end on this dark note, but sets the scene for all that God himself would do through his Son, Jesus Christ (the focus of section two), to put things right.

2

Making Sense of the Here and Now

As I sit down to write this chapter in which we reflect on the question of where we as human beings really belong, our family is waiting to take possession of our new home in Wales. Almost a year ago we watched the contents of our last home being loaded into a shipping container as we prepared to leave the United States to return to Britain. Since then, we have lived in four different temporary homes and have experienced something of what it means to be 'of no fixed abode.' That is very much what we want to consider as we trace the development of what it means to be 'resident aliens' through the unfolding message of redemption in the Bible.

In Chapter 1, we looked at what God intended for the human race in Eden and how Adam, through his rebellion, squandered God's good gift of a homeland in his presence. We saw that a major consequence of Adam's sin was to make men and women 'homeless wanderer[s] on the earth' (Gen. 4:12 NET). If we follow that motif as the drama of redemption unfolds, we discover that it has some interesting facets.

Almost immediately we see that Cain—the one God had condemned to a life of homeless wandering because of his sin against Abel—clearly found it a struggle to accept that judgement. Just a few verses later we are told that Cain 'built a city' (Gen. 4:17). Despite his sin and despite the fact he knew that God's sentence upon him was just, he longed for permanence: a place where he and his family could belong.

This same thought sits quietly under the surface of the ensuing chapters (Gen. 4:17–6:8), which cover the vast sweep of the early history of the human race (particularly in the refrain of Gen. 5 'and he died'), through the chaos that led up to the great flood in the time of Noah. Through that deluge, God, in effect, washes his world clean, giving Noah and his family a fresh start. It was not 'redemption' in the form humanity ultimately needed it, because Noah, though rescued, still rebelled in a shameful and tragic fashion (Gen. 9:21). But it showed the innate sinfulness that, by virtue of his being the covenant head of the whole human race (Rom. 5:12), Adam had bequeathed to his wife and descendants was still present.

The following chapters chart the nations that descended from Noah and his sons and the next big event-horizon we encounter as those nations multiply is the building of the Tower of Babel (Gen. 11:1-9). Man's motive behind this vast enterprise in structural engineering was to 'make a name for ourselves, lest we be dispersed over the face of the whole earth' (Gen. 11:4). God's words condemning Cain to a restless existence are echoed in these words of his distant relatives. And just as Cain sought to counter them by building a city, so those who followed him sought to establish a spiritual citadel for themselves. Their plans, however, were crushed. God's response to this act of mass mutiny was to do the very thing humanity had sought to avoid: 'the LORD dispersed them from there over the face of all the earth, and they left off building the city' (Gen. 11:8).

The Babel instinct in the human psyche has lingered on through the entire history of our race. From man's attempts to literally 'build a name for himself' by constructing great works of architectural genius, to his efforts to establish kingdoms and empires, human beings have tried to secure themselves in this world through all manner of tangible means. It can be seen not just in the realm of power politics and the corporate world, but also right down to family life and even our own individual existence. We try to build our own little worlds without God through our careers, achievements, acquisitions, families, and other things in the vain hope they will provide the security and sense of identity we crave. But, just as it was then, our efforts to establish our own security are futile.

The Babel story provides a major punctuation mark in the Genesis record. It encapsulates the extent to which paradise was indeed lost through Adam's fall on a scale that would literally have global, indeed cosmic, proportions. But then we meet Abraham (who was called Abram at that time), and through him are allowed to see the scope and scale of the salvation God had planned for the world (Gen. 12:1-3). Very quickly, as we get into the account of God's dealings with Abraham, we discover that the question of finding a permanent home is still very much to the fore. However, there are some twists and turns that we, perhaps, do not expect. And that is what we will explore in the next few chapters.

3

From Nomads to a Nation

THE Babel fiasco in Genesis, which we looked at in the previous chapter, is quickly followed in the timeline of salvation by the account of Abraham (from Gen. 12). This looks very much like a ray of light into what otherwise seems to be a very dark world. It especially looks this way because God explicitly tells him he would give his descendants the land of Canaan (Gen. 12:7). But there is something of a twist in the tale: Abraham already had an apparently secure and comfortable home in Ur of the Chaldeans. Why, then, does an act of trusting obedience to God mean leaving this home, for him and his immediate family to spend the rest of their earthly lives as nomads on the earth?

In order to begin to answer this question, we need to skip ahead in the Bible's storyline to the book of Hebrews, which makes reference to Abraham and his willingness to accept the nomadic life to which God called him. It says, 'they [Abraham and his family] desire a better country, that is, a heavenly one' (Heb. 11:16). We will look at the Hebrews angle in more detail in the fifth chapter, but for now we simply note that Abraham did not begrudge this calling from God.

Indeed, the gift of Canaan to Abraham's descendants would not physically happen until some five hundred years after Abraham's death. During that time, not only would the patriarchs continue in the nomadic existence of their forefather, but their descendants would spend several centuries as an enslaved people in a foreign land in Egypt. Then, even after their departure from Egypt under the leadership of Moses, an entire generation would spend forty years as wilderness wanderers before the Land of Promise became the land of their actual possession.

So we have this long period, covering numerous generations during which God's covenant people—the very people to whom God promised salvation—continued to experience their own brand of 'homeless wandering on the earth.' Their heart instinct for a place of permanence was still eluding them.

This monumental detail, which can so easily be overlooked as we try to assimilate God's unfolding purpose in redemption, says a great deal about where the focus of redemption lies. Although the human heart longs for 'deliverance' in some form of heaven on earth, it cannot be on earth as we know it. Even the life of faith will be a life filled with restlessness so long as we are in this world. This is why Abraham's act of obedience meant spending the rest of his life as a nomad on the earth: he was pursuing a better country, a heavenly one.

Significantly, we continue to see this life of restlessness when the Israelites enter Canaan. The overwhelming sense of awe and anticipation that travelled with them across the Jordan into what was about to become *their* land (Josh. 3:1-17), very quickly dissipates in the chapters and indeed the books of the Bible that follow. The residue of the Joshua narrative is one of battle and conflict to secure the borders of Israel and, despite what feels like an all-too-brief moment of peace and stability in the land, it immediately gives way to Judges and the anarchy and chaos that threatens to tear apart the fragile nation of Israel.

The little book of Ruth, to some, may seem difficult to make sense of sandwiched, as it is, between Judges and the books of Samuel. But it once more picks up on the theme of restlessness in this present life. It gives a glimpse in microcosm of a displaced Israelite family that came back to their homeland after years of self-inflicted exile, only to face an uncertain future in Israel. However, far from being a whimsical interlude to the record of God's saving purpose, it provides the next link in the chain—reaffirming God's saving promise to his people through Ruth's link with King David (Ruth 4:18-22).

In Samuel, Kings, and Chronicles, even with the establishment of the monarchy in Israel—which had the potential under God of securing the homeland—it was only the golden age of the Davidic reign that showed any kind of promise. The kingdom quickly split in two, and the kings that 'did what was evil in the sight of the LORD' vastly outnumbered the faithful ones.

The final punctuation mark in this saga of the People of God is exile. It would be permanent exile in the case of the Northern Kingdom and a seventy-year exile for Judah. In both cases it was an expression of the ultimate sanction, after years of covenant infidelity (Deut. 28:58, 63). And even though a small but faithful remnant would return under Ezra and Nehemiah, their spiritual fortunes are at best volatile and, post-Malachi, they descend into a four-hundred-year spiritual black hole between the Testaments.

What was Israel meant to make of this, and what are we to make of it all? A mere surface reading of this theme as it is woven through Old Testament revelation might suggest that the thought of a home that would replace the lost home of Eden was a wonderful dream in the promise of redemption, but one which turned into an abject failure. A careful reading of the text, however,—especially one that leads us into the New Testament—shows this is anything but the case. Indeed, God in his wise and loving purpose was impressing deeply on his believing people that this world in its present fallen state can never provide the home that we need and for which we were uniquely formed as human beings.

That same Old Testament reality is repeated in the New Testament, as we shall see in the next chapter, and is also one that we need to grasp. It is all-too-easy for God's believing people through the ages to subliminally embrace a hope of heaven-on-this-earth, which can simply never happen in God's economy of grace. He has planned something *better by far* for all who trust him!

4

The Homeless Jesus

I WAS talking recently with a dear friend who had been going through significant housing issues with all the mental, emotional and spiritual turmoil that came with them. But then she interjected, 'I suddenly realised, Jesus didn't have a home.' She was absolutely right. Our Lord himself summed up his earthly experience with the words, 'Foxes have holes, and birds of the air have nests, but the Son of Man has nowhere to lay his head' (Luke 9:58). Even though, in the immediate context, he was referring to the itinerant nature of his three-year public ministry; in another sense it summed up his entire earthly existence. From his birth in some kind of outhouse in Bethlehem to his body being laid in borrowed tomb after his death, his resident status was chequered to say the least.

In Matthew's record of the nativity, we are told that after the visit of the Magi and a warning from an angel, Mary and Joseph, and the infant Jesus, became asylum-seekers in Egypt for an unspecified length of time. Despite the added trauma this brought into Mary and Joseph's already traumatic life, Matthew adds a little note to his account, showing that this was not some unexpected interruption to God's redemptive purpose, but a necessary component of the deliverance Christ had come to secure. He says, quoting the prophet Hosea (11:1), 'This was to fulfil what the Lord had spoken by the prophet, "Out of Egypt I called my son"' (Matt. 2:15). Here is not the place to delve into the intricacies of Matthew's choice and handling of the Hosea text; here it will suffice to say that Jesus' deliverance out of an Egyptian bondage as a toddler was bound up with the extent of his identification with those he came to save. From the very inception in his earthly life he entered into their displacement in order to initiate the restoration that they needed.

The thirty or so years of silence that follow gloss over, almost without comment, the time Jesus spent in Nazareth. Although it is clear that those were years when Jesus did have a home—and was there long enough to earn the epithet, 'the carpenter's son' (Matt. 13:55)—nevertheless, as David E. Garland notes in his commentary on Luke, in the eyes of Jesus' contemporaries, Nazareth was synonymous with 'Nowhereville'! Then, from the point when Jesus formally commenced his public ministry to the end of his life, he was 'on the road.' He called his followers to leave their livelihoods (Mark 1:16-20; 2:14) in order to be his disciples, and they did.

Throughout his ministry we see him dependent upon the kindness of others, such as the women mentioned in Luke, for his support (Luke 8:3). We see him looking forward to staying with people, like Mary, Martha and Lazarus, who regularly gave him a bed for the night. In the very last week leading up to his arrest and crucifixion, we see him having to borrow a large upstairs room in someone's house in Jerusalem in order to celebrate the Passover with the twelve (Mark 14:15). And, as we have noted already, even in his death he had no grave of his own in which his body could be laid; that too had to be loaned by Joseph of Arimathea (Mark 15:46).

So, in a very real and deliberate sense, Jesus is presented to us in the Gospels as the homeless one. His thirty years residency in Nazareth is glossed over as insignificant in the larger framework of God's plan of salvation.

In Hebrews, we read that Jesus 'had to be made like his brothers [and sisters] in every respect, so that he might become a merciful and faithful high priest in the service of God, to make propitiation for the sins of the people' (Heb. 2:17). This helps us to grasp what is going on. It was necessary for him, as the God-appointed head and representative of his people, that he should enter fully into the human condition in order to rescue them from it 'to the uttermost' (Heb. 7:25). This means it was necessary for Jesus to enter into the part of human experience which is being a homeless wanderer on the earth.

It was necessary, in part, for him to do this in order to bring about a genuine rescue. He had to plumb the very depths of what 'lostness' entails, and this he did in his cry of forsakenness on the cross. That instant, which marked the nadir of his redemptive sufferings, is something we can but observe from afar and view in grateful wonder. While we are unable to comprehend it, we joyfully embrace it as the turning-point of destiny. The downward trajectory of Christ's suffering on the cross turned upward at that point, marking the moment in history at which the hell-ward trajectory of our sin-cursed world was reversed. The saviour of the world died on a Roman gibbet, on a garbage heap outside Jerusalem, homeless, unclothed and possession-less. He did this that he might genuinely be able to say, 'I go to prepare a place for you... that where I am you may be also' (John 14:1-4). The cross was what it cost to provide a 'forever-home' for all who trust him.

The other reason why it was necessary for Jesus to be made like his brothers and sisters in this, as much as every other facet, of their experience was that he could have genuine empathy for them in their ongoing struggle (Heb. 4:14-16). He knows our anguish because he has experienced it for himself, and when he prays for us in our distress, he prays with knowledge and understanding.

So we see that we were made for something better than this current world. This is true, not just for my dear friends who were enduring a temporary displacement in life, but also for every human who struggles with the unsettledness of life, even when it ought to feel settled. In the next chapter we will return to this theme for one last time and see, in the words of Derek Thomas, 'how the gospel takes us all the way home.'

5

This World Is Not My Home

WE started in the garden of Eden and have traced out how Adam forfeited the perfect home God had given him by rebelling against God. We saw too that the divine judgement pronounced on Adam's son, Cain, after his sin of fratricide—that he would thereafter be 'a homeless wanderer on the earth' (Gen. 4:12 NET)—encapsulates the tragic reality of what Adam brought upon himself, his family and ultimately the entire human race. We are alienated from God, from each other, from our environment, and even from ourselves. Regardless of how deeply we try to sink our roots into this world, we cannot escape the overwhelming sense of futility that haunts our existence here.

What is fascinating, however, is that even for those who find the new life promised in the gospel, this restlessness remains. Yet this is no accident, Christ himself embraced it as a necessary element of his existence in this fallen world as the new and true head and representative of our race.

Our goal in this final chapter of section one is to see how this theme is further developed and explained in the rest of the New Testament and how it can only have its denouement and resolution in the new world which Christ himself will usher in upon his return.

The apostle Paul was deeply conscious of the tension Christians experience in this life; tension which is found in what has often been described as 'the already, but not yet' component of the Christian life. The 'already' aspect lies in the fact that, in Christ, we already have one foot firmly planted in heaven. As Paul reminds the Ephesians, God has already 'seated us with him [Christ] in the heavenly places in Christ Jesus' (Eph. 2:6) and they (and all Christians) are already 'blessed… with every spiritual blessing' in him (Eph. 1:3). We hold title to all Christ came to secure for his people through redemption. Yet, at the same time we are 'not yet' what we ought to be. God has begun 'a good work' in us, but it is not yet completed (Phil. 1:6). We live in a world that is hostile to God and to his people—one in which we 'are always being given over to death for Jesus' sake' (2 Cor. 4:11). Like Paul, we find ourselves being torn between wanting to depart this world and be with Christ, which is 'far better' (Phil. 1:23) and remaining in this world to serve him.

In his letter to the Philippians, playing on the fact this city was a Roman colony, Paul says, 'But our citizenship is in heaven' (Phil. 3:20). Yes, we may have a passport for whatever nation into which we were born (or chose to adopt), but that is not where our real citizenship is located. Albert Edward Brumley captured this thought somewhat quaintly, but in a way that has struck a chord with many Christians, in the words of the gospel song, 'This World Is Not My Home':

This world is not my home, I'm just a passing through;
  My treasures are laid up somewhere beyond the blue:
The angels beckon me from heaven's open door,
  And I can't feel at home in this world anymore.

For Brumley, these words were penned out of the context of his upbringing in the poverty of Mid-America in the 1920s and the Great Depression that followed. His Christian faith gave him a different perspective on the hardships that surrounded him and the hope of that better world that God has promised to his people.

In the General Epistles, some of which were written against the backdrop of the Christian Diaspora that resulted from waves of Jewish and Roman persecutions, this thought is presented with an even greater poignancy. As we saw in an earlier chapter, Peter uses the language of displaced persons when he addresses the scattered believers of his day as those who are 'strangers in the world' scattered throughout the Roman provinces (1 Pet. 1:1 NIV). Later he calls them to live like 'aliens and strangers' in this world as they consciously abstain from the corrupt behaviour that is its hallmark (1 Pet. 2:11 NIV)—saying, in effect, 'we don't belong here!'

It is, however, the book of Hebrews that captures the deepest sense in which every true Christian lives with tension so long as they remain in this world. Summing up how we as Christians are to cope with the exigencies, or demands, of the life of faith in the here and now, he says, 'For here we have no lasting city, but we seek the city that is to come' (Heb. 13:14). Like our spiritual ancestors cited in the eleventh chapter of Hebrews, we 'desire a better country, that is, a heavenly one'

(Heb. 11:16), we desire 'the city that has foundations, whose designer and builder is God' (Heb. 11:10).

There is solidity to the prospect of the everlasting home Christ is preparing for his people that has too often been lost in evangelical preaching. The notion of 'heaven' as our everlasting home has, for many Christians, been one of a disembodied existence in an ethereal world. But that is far-removed from what we find in Scripture. Peter encourages his readers by saying that although 'the heavens will pass away with a roar, and the heavenly bodies will be burned up and dissolved, and the earth and the works that are done on it will be exposed' (2 Pet. 3:10), 'according to his [God's] promise we are waiting for new heavens and a new earth in which righteousness dwells' (2 Pet. 3:13). That new world order will be every bit as tangible and colourful as the broken order we have left behind.

So, therein lies the ultimate journey that takes us, in the words of John Milton, from 'Paradise Lost' to 'Paradise Regained.' And the essence of this paradise is 'at-home-ness.' This is infinitely more than just having somewhere to live; it is to have a 'house' turned into a 'home' because of who we share it with. Adam (and through him, humanity) was never made to be 'alone'—not just because of his need of a human counterpart and companion, but ultimately because he was made by God and for God, to ever live in fellowship with God. That's why Moses so eloquently states, 'Lord, you have been our dwelling place in all generations' (Psa. 90:1).

What about the home that Christ is preparing for his people—this paradise he has promised for their future? Will it just be a reinstatement of what Adam lost in Eden? No! As Isaac Watts puts it in his rendition of Psalm 72:

> Where He [Christ] displays His healing power,
>   Death and the curse are known no more:
> In Him the tribes of Adam boast
>   More blessings than their father lost.

The 'more blessings than our father lost' of which he speaks points to the fact we will not be on probation in heaven—living under a huge question mark of whether or not we will be allowed to stay. This is because, just as Adam was acting not merely for himself, but others also, so too was Jesus. He has fulfilled all righteousness for all his people and he has accomplished all that was required to secure this everlasting home for all who trust him. For those of us who trust and follow him, let us rejoice. For those who have yet to believe, hear the words of Jesus: 'Come to me, all who labour and are heavy laden, and I will give you rest' (Matt. 11:28). He calls us to come home forever!

Section Two

Christ: the Pioneer and Perfecter of Salvation

Therefore, since we are surrounded by so great a cloud of witnesses, let us also lay aside every weight, and sin which clings so closely, and let us run with endurance the race that is set before us, looking to Jesus, the founder and perfecter of our faith, who for the joy that was set before him endured the cross, despising the shame, and is seated at the right hand of the throne of God.

Consider him who endured from sinners such hostility against himself, so that you may not grow weary or faint-hearted.

Hebrews 12:1-3

6

Who Is Jesus Christ?

LIFE and relationships have become all too superficial in our present age. It is the easiest thing in the world to say we know someone and yet really have nothing more than a nodding acquaintance. Indeed, with the influence of the media—television in particular—it is possible to see some famous personality on the street and instinctively feel that we know them, even though we have never even met them. They are really complete strangers to us. Sadly, the same can be true of our reaction to the greatest person ever to step on to the stage of human history—the Lord Jesus Christ. The critical difference about our knowledge of him is that it impinges upon our eternal destiny. Thus, one of the most penetrating questions a person can ask in life is, 'Who *is* Jesus Christ?'

At one level it is a question for those who have had little or no exposure to the Christian faith, either in terms of its teaching, or its practice in the life of those who are Christians. Historically, the heart of a missionary's work entailed presenting and explaining Jesus to people in other cultures who had never heard his name before. But even today, in countries that once had a Christian heritage, there are many people who really have no idea who he is or why he came. Our own secularised western world is full of people for whom 'Jesus Christ' is nothing more than a profanity. The church has a mission field on its own doorstep.

At another level it is also a question for those who claim to be believers, but for whom Christianity is nothing more than a label that they have applied to themselves. They really need to ask themselves some probing questions about the way Jesus affects the way they live and how they worship. Paul's warnings about a faith that is all form and no content (2 Tim. 3:5) are real—the dangers of a Christ-less Christianity are too serious to contemplate.

Jesus himself provides the bottom line on the issues that are at stake. As he prepares for his ultimate ordeal on the cross and is engaged in prayer beforehand, he declares to his heavenly father, 'this is eternal life, that they may know you, the only true God, and Jesus Christ whom you have sent' (John 17:3). The very essence of eternal life is to know God through Jesus Christ his Son. To know him, not merely in terms of being able to pass examinations on him, but to know him in the most intimate and life-changing fashion. Then we will find that the answer to our question about Jesus is really the answer to the question of life itself.

Who, then, is this Jesus, and what is it about him uniquely that makes him the pivot on which the destiny of all men turns? One of the most concise, yet pointed answers is to be found in the *Apostles' Creed*. There we find five axiomatic truths about the identity of Jesus, each of which underpin the work he came to do.

In the first place, he is the eternal Son: 'I believe... in Jesus Christ his [God, the Father Almighty's] only begotten Son...' To begin to understand Jesus, we cannot start in time, but rather eternity and the mystery of God himself. Throughout the Old Testament God made himself known as the one true God who is one and who alone is to be worshipped by all creation (Deut. 6:4; Isa. 45:5). He is the God of all creation who would brook no rivals. Yet, intriguingly, he made himself known to the world in a way that suggested there was more to his oneness than met the eye. Right at the very beginning of the Bible in the account of creation there are several details that are at the very least unusual. The Hebrew word for God is plural in form, yet is used with singular Hebrew verb forms (Gen. 1:1). When he comes to create man, he enters into consultation and using plural Hebrew verbs says, 'Let *us* make man in *our* image...' (Gen. 1:26), as opposed to 'Let *me*... in *my*...' (the pronouns being encoded in the Hebrew verbs). These details in themselves prove nothing, but in the light of later revelation they seem to hint at the fact that the God who is one, is also the God who is three. He exists in everlasting Trinity: God the Father, God the Son and God the Holy Spirit.

The significance of the second person of the Trinity is highlighted sharply by the apostle John in his Gospel where he starts his account of Jesus with the words, 'In the beginning was the Word' (John 1:1). The 'Word' who 'became flesh and dwelt among us' (John 1:14) was none other than

Jesus of Nazareth, the Christ of God. He was the one who himself was profoundly conscious of the glory that was inherently his, which was veiled from human eyes during his time on earth, yet would be restored when his work on earth was done (John 17:5).

To know Jesus is to know God. It is to be face to face with the one whose identity lies in eternity and whose power and glory towers over all. He takes our breath away, as he does with the angels of heaven, as the one who is worthy of all praise. He captures our hearts as the one who alone is worthy of our trust. The other gods of the world speak about salvation, but only in terms of telling men what they must do to save themselves. The God of the Bible speaks about salvation and tells the world what he himself has done to bring it (John 3:16).

In the second place, Jesus is also the incarnate Lord. The way in which the divine intervention took place is almost too much for words to express. God became man. The infinite stepped into the finite. The creator took upon himself the flesh of his creature. To think that this began in the unique miracle of conception that occurred in the womb of a young girl from an obscure village in Palestine only serves to magnify the wonder of what happened. It was not merely, in the words of Charles Wesley, that Jesus was 'Our God contracted to a span,' but rather to a tiny cluster of dividing cells in a woman's body. He 'made himself nothing... being born in the likeness of men' (Phil. 2:7). He was 'conceived of the Holy Ghost; born of the Virgin Mary' (*Apostle's Creed*). Such was the need of those he came to save that 'he had to be made like his brothers in every respect' (Heb. 2:17). If he, as the 'second man' and 'last Adam' (1 Cor. 15:45, 47) was going to undo the damage done to humanity and to creation by the father of the race, then he had to actually take real human nature in order to redeem it.

There is a strong temptation to play down the genuineness of Christ's humanity by always seeing it as overshadowed by his deity. Yet he was truly a man among men. He knew what it was to be hungry (Matt. 4:2), thirsty (John 19:28), weary (John 4:6) and at times even ignorant of facts (Mark 5:30), and all of this had a unique contribution to make to the greatness of his redemption. The writer to the Hebrews draws it out graphically, writing to Christians who thought no-one could feel for them in their plight, by pointing to Jesus, their great high priest who is truly able to sympathise with those in need and extend the help most suited to their circumstances (Heb. 4:14-16).

By becoming incarnate, Jesus bridged the great divide between a holy heaven and a fallen earth. In his person, he joined humanity and deity in an eternal union that would have eternal implications for all who come to him by faith.

Thirdly, Jesus is presented in Scripture as the suffering servant. As great as the incarnation was, it was not in itself sufficient to redeem a lost humanity. For the saviour to save, it was necessary for him to suffer. Thus, in the words of the *Apostles' Creed*, we confess that Jesus, 'suffered under Pontius Pilate, was crucified, dead and buried; he descended into hell.' He was none other than the suffering servant of the

Lord predicted by Isaiah (52:13–53:12) almost seven hundred years beforehand.

He came not only as Priest whose job it was to offer sacrifice for the sins of the people, but also as Sacrifice—the only sacrifice that could ever satisfy God's perfect requirements for perfect atonement (Heb. 9:14). He faced head-on the sobering fact of divine justice that, 'without the shedding of blood there is no forgiveness' (Heb. 9:22).

The whole concept of atonement by bloody sacrifice has been deemed the ultimate in political incorrectness, not just in recent times, but also for the past two centuries and beyond. For many, a bloodless Christianity is the only kind of palatable Christianity. They are quite content to admire Jesus as their great role model, listen to him as their great teacher, but they will not look to him as the one who took their place.

The cross has never been a part of the gospel with which people can feel comfortable. Even in Paul's day it was a scandal for some and a laughing-stock for others (1 Cor. 1:23). Yet without it there could have been no salvation. Jesus could not have uttered the most critical words of his entire mission, 'It is finished' (John 19:30), nor looked upon the travail of his soul and been satisfied (Isa. 53:11).

In his death, he not only descended into the place the Greeks called 'Hades'—the realm of the dead—but, as many understand the statement in the *Apostles' Creed* to mean, he plumbed the very depths of hell itself in the place of sinners who deserve it. In that moment, which has become the very turning point of history, Jesus, in his body, was sacrificed 'once for all' in the place of his people (Heb. 10:10). As Peter told the scattered church of his day, 'Christ also suffered once for sins, the righteous for the unrighteous, that he might bring us to God' (1 Pet. 3:18). His sufferings were for his people's salvation.

In the fourth place, Jesus is also the exalted saviour. There has been much debate among theological specialists as to which truth lies at the very heart of the gospel. Some have argued, for the kind of reasons outlined above, that it must be the cross. Paul seems to summarise his entire ministry with the words, 'I decided to know nothing among you except Jesus Christ and him crucified' (1 Cor. 2:2). And yet the balance of Paul's recorded ministry in the epistles seems to focus more upon the resurrection of Jesus. The solution to the problem is not to exalt one above the other, but to recognise that it is impossible to have one without the other. The cross would have been a failure without the resurrection and the resurrection would be meaningless without the cross. Hence the next great affirmation about Christ which is found in the creed declares, 'the third day, he rose from the dead; he ascended into heaven; and is seated at the right hand of God the Father Almighty.'

As we try to understand who Jesus is and what he has accomplished in redemption, we not only see him in his pre-existent glory, follow him into the downward spiral of his humiliation, into the depths of punitive torment, but we ultimately watch him soar in exaltation to the place of highest honour in heaven (Heb. 12:2). The exaltation of Jesus does not merely consist of what took place from the point he was taken up into heaven before the eyes of the disciples (Acts 1:9), but from before that, having its roots in the miracle of the resurrection. Paul tells the Christians at Rome that it was through the resurrection that Jesus 'was declared to be the Son of God in power' by the Holy Spirit (Rom. 1:4). The glory, which had been veiled in human flesh throughout his life and ministry on earth, was, in the resurrection and during the forty days that followed, revealed in the new body Jesus displayed when he emerged from the tomb. The significance of that event and that special body is something that Paul latches onto and expounds in his first letter to the Corinthians.

In First Corinthians, he argues with those who doubt the very idea of resurrection in principle by saying, 'if Christ has not been raised, then our preaching is in vain and your faith is in vain' (1 Cor. 15:14). It is a crucial element to the Christian gospel and to Christian faith. The glory of the message hangs upon the glory of what really happened. It is nothing short of the glory of final victory—death has in truth been defeated, the powers of the grave vanquished. More than that, the character of Christ's resurrection body —with the obvious glory that attaches to it—becomes the prototype of the bodies that the saints will have after his return (1 Cor. 15:35-57).

This great truth gives a new and intriguing twist to our understanding of who Jesus is: he is the one who has already taken human flesh to glory. When he returned to the place of honour at his Father's right hand, he did not cease to be man or abandon his flesh; he took his humanity with him as he 'passed through the heavens' (Heb. 4:14). To borrow Rabbi Duncan's phrase, 'there is dust of the earth in heaven for us.' Although there are saints in glory at this moment, they are disembodied spirits (Heb. 12:23). The only flesh in that wonderful place is the flesh of Jesus. It is there—he is there—as the living guarantee that all who put their faith in him will one day be raised from death as he was and taken to the glory where he is (1 Cor. 15:20).

The exaltation of Christ provides not only the pattern, but also the assurance of the future exaltation of our humanity that was debased by the fall. Only as we are found in him can we have our human dignity truly restored and reinstated to the glory for which it was intended. The glory which we receive from him when we first share in his resurrection life is but a foretaste of the glory that will be ours when he comes to lift us from our graves and take us home to a glorified world and universe.

Ultimately, Jesus is the coming judge of all the earth. It is that future day of his return that provides the final clue to the identity of Jesus and the reason we must trust him. Right now he is enthroned at the right hand of his Father and 'from there he shall come to judge the living and the dead' (*Apostles' Creed*). It is the risen, exalted reality of Christ that not only provides hope and comfort for all who trust him, but also should strike fear into those who do not. Paul uses the twin truths of resurrection and exaltation to buttress the great command of the gospel that 'all people everywhere' repent (Acts 17:30). For those who refuse to do so, they will discover to their cost that the very one they have rejected is the one to whom they must answer as their judge.

Who, then, is this Jesus? He is Son of God and Son of Man, saviour of his people, and judge of all the earth. He is the one to whom we must go by faith if we are to escape the judgment which is to come and find an everlasting home in God's New Creation.

7

The Incarnation: Glimpsing Mystery

ADVENT is the season when the church around the world celebrates the birth of our Lord. It is a season with an interesting and uneven pedigree, not to mention a few curiosities and anomalies. Perhaps the greatest anomaly is that the focus on Bethlehem as the place of birth of the incarnate Christ has managed to obscure where the heart of this mystery really lies.

The place in which this miracle of miracles occurred was in Nazareth; or, more specifically, in the womb of the virgin Mary in Nazareth. The exact moment it took place we do not know. We do have, however, a measured insight into the manner in which this extraordinary event happened in Gabriel's answer to Mary's question, 'How will this be, since I am a virgin?' (Luke 1:34, 35). However, before Mary's question, Gabriel indicated that the son she bore would be no ordinary child. He would be 'great' and would be called 'Jesus' [the Lord saves]; he would also be called, 'Son of the Most High' and be given 'the throne of his father David' and 'of his kingdom there will be no end' (Luke 1:31-33). All of these clues clearly point to greatness, but not necessarily a greatness that could not be contained in a human individual with unusual gifts and capacity.

Mary's concern, however, hinges on her virgin state, and clearly the very thought of seeking fulfilment of this promise through natural intercourse was nowhere in her mind. Indeed, everything about her angelic encounter pointed to there being something of hitherto unknown greatness unfolding before her eyes. Gabriel makes it clear that this is in fact the case as he answers her: 'The Holy Spirit will come upon you, and the power of the Most High will overshadow you; therefore the child to be born will be called holy—the Son of God' (Luke 1:35). This was territory that no rabbi, theologian or prophet had seriously contemplated before, but was being revealed to an insignificant Galilean girl by one of the ambassadors of heaven.

There is no indication that the miraculous conception occurred at that moment. All we are told is Mary's response to the announcement: 'I am the servant of the Lord; let it be to me according to your word' (Luke 1:38). It is, without question, utterly appropriate that this should have been the case. The intimacy as much as the mystery of any conception deserves privacy, how much more then, the unfathomable mystery of what happened in Mary's womb. (Something that is counterbalanced by the privacy that shrouds the resurrection in the darkness of the tomb at the other end of Christ's earthly life.) That it did happen is simply a matter of fact as Luke goes on to record the encounter between the pregnant Elizabeth, Mary's near relative, and what was clearly the pregnant Mary (Luke 1:39-45). But Luke takes us no further in understanding what happened in that moment of enfleshment when the eternal Son of God took the DNA of Mary to become the perfect representative of humanity.

Indeed, apart from John in his prologue, the Gospel writers add almost nothing to what we have in Luke. However, we are given a profound glimpse of the mystery of what was involved in the incarnation in a very unlikely portion of the New Testament in a somewhat surprising context. The context is a church which, on the surface of things, appears as perhaps the most attractive church in the New Testament world: the church in Philippi, addressed by Paul in a letter which has often been dubbed 'the Epistle of Joy.' At face value it may well have seemed like a joyful congregation, but as its founding apostle begins to peel back some of the layers in its life, he soon exposes some sad and painful realities. In particular, he identifies 'rivalry' and 'conceit' as two of the cardinal sins lurking in its pews and traces their source to the idolatry of self-interest (Phil. 2:3, 4).

Although they may fall into the category of what Jerry Bridges calls, 'respectable sins,' they are among the most insidious sins that can infect the body of Christ. Not only do they lie behind the most devastating divisions the church can suffer, but they invariably distort and discredit the gospel before a watching world. The depth of the serious-ness of these sins is reflected in the fact that Paul reaches for the most heavyweight ordnance in his theological arsenal to address them. He reaches for the doctrine of the incarnation in a way that takes us deeper into what it entails than anywhere else in Scripture.

Having just exhorted his listeners with the words, 'Your attitude should be the same as that of Christ Jesus,' he then says of Christ, 'who, though he was in the form of God, did not count equality with God a thing to be grasped, but made himself nothing, taking the form of a servant, being born in the likeness of men. And being found in human form, he humbled himself by becoming obedient to the point of death, even death on a cross' (Phil. 2:6-8).

The controlling thought in this extended statement about Christ is that he 'made himself nothing' (Phil. 2:7)—it is the idea of *kenosis. Kenosis* is a concept that has stretched the minds of commentators and theologians through the ages. In what sense can the one who is Lord of all and who the heavens cannot contain be said to 'make himself nothing'? There have been some notoriously wrong answers, like that of Charles Wesley's 'emptied himself of all but love.' And there have been some radical attempts to explain it, as with the kenotic theories of the Higher Critical schools of nineteenth century Germany that suggested that the Son somehow divested himself of some or all of the attributes of deity. (These theories inevitably imploded—unable to sustain internal consistency as a meaningful description of Christ as the God-man.)

How, then, are we to understand what *kenosis* entailed for Christ? Although from the context of what Paul is saying, it clearly has a bearing on all that Christ became and accomplished to secure redemption, it has its roots in and emanates from the moment of his incarnation. It was at that moment in time when, 'What he was, he continued to be; what he was not, he took to himself' (Gregory of Nazianzus, Oration 29.19).

Paul does not so much delve into the ontology of the incarnation in his statement as to the 'attitude' that made Christ willing to undergo this extraordinary addition—the attitude that was to reshape that of the Philippians (Phil. 2:5). It was an attitude that enabled him to not grasp on to the 'equality with God' that was and always had been rightfully his (Phil. 2:6). Understanding what it meant hinges on how we understand the word *morphe* (Phil. 2:6, 7), literally translated 'form' in ESV, NRSV, and NASB, but translated 'very nature' in the NIV, reflecting a specific interpretative decision on the part of its translators. Donald Macleod argues helpfully for the retention of 'form' as preferable because Paul's use of 'form' is the hinge on which his whole argument turns in this passage.[1] He highlights the nuance in 'form' that has to do with how someone or something is perceived—regardless of the underlying reality. Macleod's reason for pressing this point is that the Philippians were not being asked to undergo a change in their being; but rather, to consciously change their attitude to one another.

How does the *kenosis* of Christ help them to grasp this point? By appreciating the fact that Jesus, throughout the entire journey that led him from glory to Golgotha, allowed himself to be misperceived—even by those he came to

[1] D. Macleod, *The Person and Work of Christ* (Leicester: IVP, 1998), pp. 205-20.

save. Furthermore, he did so by not standing on his rights. Indeed, by adopting the posture of a bond-slave (Phil. 2:7) and placing himself under the divine anathema through 'death on a cross' (Phil. 2:8), he allowed surface perception to almost totally obscure the sheer wonder of who he really was, and what he was actually doing. He made himself nothing in the eyes of men, that all who trust him might have everything in fellowship with God.

Kenosis is but one facet of the mystery of what happened in Nazareth; but it is no small facet. By deigning to take our humanity to himself in the way he did, in the virgin Mary of Nazareth's womb, meant that he grew up with the stigma of perceived illegitimacy hanging over him. He also grew up in poverty and obscurity, and when he began his earthly ministry this was compounded by the contempt of his family and fellow villagers. When he prayed in Gethsemane, 'My Father, if it be possible, let this cup pass from me' (Matt. 26:39), as Sinclair Ferguson has observed, he was not having a crisis of faith, but was praying the only way he could pray under the circumstances. As the one who had kept the law in its totality and fulfilled all righteousness, 'the cup' of the cross that loomed over him was unreasonable and unjust for himself personally (though not for those he came to represent). Nevertheless—in line with his *kenotic* spirit—he adds his own 'nevertheless' to his prayer: 'not as I will, but as you will.' And even though that would ultimately mean being anathematised on what Macleod has called 'the garbage heap of Jerusalem,' he willed that it would be so, because it was for sinners who would otherwise be anathematised that he came. Therein lies the ultimate mystery—and majesty—of the incarnation.

8

Tempted, Tried, but Never Failing

THE temptations of Christ are recorded in three out of the four Gospels, they are clearly meant to highlight a significant component of Jesus' mission to save. But, despite their prominence in the Gospels, they have been subjected to a range of interpretations—some of which tend towards misinterpretation.

The most common misinterpretation—or at least one that manages to shift the main focus of this episode away from its central significance—is to regard Jesus as a model of how to deal with temptation. So, when Satan tempts us to sin, like Jesus we should have a suitable arsenal of Bible verses at our fingertips with which to resist his overtures.

Although there is undoubtedly some truth in that approach, it fails to do justice to the passages that record this incident and the weight they attach to it. The Gospels present it as an integral part of what Jesus had to accomplish to secure redemption. Each evangelist deals with the event from a slightly different angle, but with a view to highlighting the far-reaching import not only of what Christ was exposed to in his encounter with Satan, but what he actually proved and achieved through it all. Far from being forced into a defensive mode through the devil's advances, he showed himself from the very outset to be the one God had promised to send to fulfil his promise to the serpent, Satan, in the *protoevangelium* (Gen. 3:15)—God's first announcement of the gospel in Scripture.

Luke's account provides some penetrating insights into the way this episode in Jesus' personal history becomes a vital component of redemptive history. A number of details bring this into focus for us.

Luke (in line with Matthew and Mark) points to the fact that Jesus went into the wilderness because the Holy Spirit led him (Luke 4:1), but he adds one significant detail: Jesus was 'full of the Holy Spirit.' Luke, more than any other Gospel writer, has a special interest in the role of the Holy Spirit in the life and ministry of Christ. From the moment and manner of his miraculous conception (Luke 1:35) through the source of the prophetic pronouncement by Zechariah (Luke 1:67) and the encounter with Simeon in the temple (Luke 2:25-27), the messianic promise of John the Baptist (Luke 3:16) and the graphic revelation of the Spirit in Jesus' baptism (Luke 3:22), the Holy Spirit is intimately involved with the mission of Christ through all its stages.

So here, as Jesus is about to be led into the wilderness, for Luke to note that he was 'full of the Holy Spirit' (Luke 4:1) signals that he is about to face something of a different order than anything he has faced so far during his earthly life. More than that, rather than merely saying (like Matthew and Mark) that Jesus was led 'into' the desert by the Spirit, Luke writes that he was led 'in' the desert, pointing to his ongoing support throughout the wilderness ordeal.

Another significant detail is found in the name of Jesus' tempter, 'the devil' (*diabolos*; Luke 4:2). The name 'devil' (and the Hebrew form, Satan) carries the connotation of 'slanderer' and suggests that the evil one's intent through this encounter was to discredit Jesus on the very threshold of his mission and so sabotage the mission as a whole.

The reference to Jesus' being in the desert 'for forty days' in this context would also not have slipped the attention of a first century reader of the Gospel—certainly not one who was familiar with the Hebrew Bible, as Theophilus, the first recipient of this Gospel almost certainly would have been. The recurring references in the Old Testament to 'forty' periods of time—either days, years, or even the ten forties of the Egyptian captivity—almost always pointed to a significant chapter in God's programme of redemption. So at the start of the most significant chapter of all in his redemptive programme, it is hardly surprising to see that marker being laid down once more.

Perhaps the most significant detail of all that Luke gives to help us make sense of where the deeper drama lies in the temptation of Christ is found on the lips of the devil himself and the question he twice puts to Jesus: 'If you are the Son of God…' (Luke 4:3, 9). Whereas a common mistake for those who read this statement in its English translation is to assume Satan is tempting Jesus to doubt who he really is, the opposite is actually the case. If he had wanted to call

Jesus' true identity into question, he would have reached for a different grammatical construction. Instead he uses a form of words that fully acknowledges who Jesus really is: the Son of God in human flesh. Indeed, the clause is better translated, not 'if...,' but 'since you are the Son of God...,' do these things.

The devil's warped intent in this exercise was not to undermine Jesus self-understanding, but to try to induce him to violate all that was bound up with his unique identity. This is seen in the very specific nature of the temptations to which our Lord was subjected.

In the temptation to turn stones into bread (Luke 4:3) Jesus was being tempted to violate his humanity. Like Moses in the desert of Sinai, Jesus had gone forty days without food and was, not surprisingly, 'hungry' (Luke 4:2), and therefore also weak and vulnerable. His hunger was as real as Moses' had been. And it was in that context the devil planted the idea that—unlike Moses—'since he was the Son of God' and not a mere human, 'Why not use your higher power?'

There would have been nothing inherently wrong in Jesus using his supernatural power to alter a material substance to provide bread. (Jesus later multiplied loaves on at least two occasions to feed vast crowds—see Mark 6:30-44; 8:1-10.) However, it would have been a violation of his unique person as the God-man to use his divine power to override his human weakness merely to gratify his own needs. It would have negated the necessity for him 'to be made like his brothers in every respect... to help those who are being tempted' (Heb. 2:17, 18).

Hence Jesus' response to the tempter, quoting from Deuteronomy: 'Man shall not live by bread alone' (Luke 4:4). The omission of 'but man lives by every word that comes from the mouth of God' (Deut. 8:3) is not an oversight on Luke's part, but an ellipsis, since the complementary clause would have been self-evident for all who were familiar with the quotation's source. Jesus' point in this response was to remind the devil there is more to life than bread. Indeed, he was saying there is something far more basic than bread at the most basic level of human existence. Namely, that we are upheld by the word of God. This word, as Geerhardus Vos points out, is the providential word by which God upholds all things (Heb. 1:3).[2] If the man Christ Jesus were to step outside that orbit, it would have been a breach of his true humanity.

In the second temptation (in Luke's order as opposed to Matthew's) when Satan 'took Jesus up' to show him 'all the kingdoms of the world in a moment of time' (Luke 4:5), Jesus is tempted to violate his calling. The temptation was tantalising. The devil claimed he was both able and willing to give Jesus 'all this authority and their glory' on condition that Jesus worship him (Luke 4:6, 7). The power of its attraction lay in fact that Jesus' mission was ultimately to save, not just Israel, but the world. And here was a route to receiving the kingdoms of the world that would avoid the anguish of the cross.

---

[2] Geerhardus Vos, *Biblical Theology* (Grand Rapids MI: Eerdmans, 1980), pp. 336-7.

Satan's claim was not devoid of truth. He had indeed, in a limited sense, been granted power and authority over this world. (In Eph. 2:2, Paul calls him 'the prince of the power of the air' indicating his sphere of influence.) But Jesus knew that to accede to his demand would have literally turned the order of creation on its head. It would have meant the creator worshipping and serving the creature. Hence his retort from Deuteronomy, 'You shall worship the Lord your God, and him only shall you serve' (Luke 4:8, quoting Deut. 6:13). Jesus refused to waver in his confidence that however painful and challenging his calling was—requiring 'becoming obedient to the point of death, even death on a cross' (Phil. 2:8)—that calling was underwritten not only by the wisdom of God, but also his perfect love.

The final temptation (in Luke's order) was designed to make Jesus violate his divine Sonship. Satan took Jesus to the highest point of the temple and urged him (with a distorted quote from Scripture) to throw himself down from there (Luke 4:9). Satan's twisted logic as he reaches for the words of Psalm 91:11, 12 infers that if God had promised the protection of angels to mere men, then how much more to the Son for whom he had so recently declared his love (Luke 3:22).

In one sense he was quite right to make such an argument. Jesus himself would tell his captors in Gethsemane that, if he so chose, he could summon 'more than twelve legions of angels' to rescue him (Matt. 26:53), but he chose not to. To do so would have been an abuse of his Sonship at that critical moment and would, at a stroke, have negated his entire role in redemption. Therefore, when Jesus responds for the last time, there is a double edge to his final quotation: 'You shall not put the Lord your God to the test' (Luke 4:12, quoting Deut. 6:16). Speaking with a profound consciousness of his being Son of God in human flesh, he looks his tempter in the eye and reminds him he is not merely testing the unseen God in heaven, but God-made-visible on earth.

What, then, are we to make of this strange, but signifi-cant episode in the life of Christ? Can we only be spectators who look on from a distance and wonder what difference it can make to us? The words of J. Wilbur Chapman's hymn, 'Jesus, What a Friend for Sinners,' may answer that for us. Speaking of our own experience as believers he says though we are, 'tempted, tried and sometimes [many times] fail-ing, He, [our] strength, [our] victory wins.' How is this so? Because he, like us, was tempted and tried; but was never failing! It is also because he was acting as our covenant head and representative—the 'second man' and the 'last Adam.' He was securing our deliverance and guaranteeing we will stand in the end. Additionally, in his office as our great high priest—being tempted in every way as we are, but without sin—he is able to sympathise with us, extend mercy when we fail, and provide the strengthening grace that helps in our time of need (Heb. 4:14-16). How else can we respond, but with the refrain:

> Hallelujah, what a Saviour!
>   Hallelujah, what a Friend!
> Saving, helping, keeping, loving;
>   He is with me to the end!

9

Gethsemane and the Mystery of the Gospel

WHAT happened in the garden of Gethsemane is an integral part of the passion narrative, but it too easily becomes incidental to the message of the gospel. All three synoptic Gospels include an account of Christ in Gethsemane in some detail, each one from a slightly different perspective. But it is easy to lose sight of the significance of what is going on in the physical and spiritual darkness of that night.

At the most basic level, it is tempting to view this merely as part of the record of events leading up to the crucifixion. In all four Gospels, the space devoted to this single week in Jesus' life and ministry (and, indeed, to the twenty-four-hour period at the end of that week) is disproportionate to the space devoted to everything else. Clearly the evangelists would have us realise that what took place in this time frame is bound up with the heart of God's good news. Since that is the case, it suggests there is more than just historical interest bound up with this level of detail: there is profound theological significance in what happens as well. We see this broadly in the way the events relating to Gethsemane are handled elsewhere in the New Testament. Thus, if we follow the axiom of Scripture being its own interpreter, this should alert us to key aspects we need to understand.

The book of Hebrews alludes to the events in the garden in at least two places. In the first, with reference to the high priestly office and ministry of Christ, the writer says:

> In the days of his flesh, Jesus offered up prayers and supplications, with loud cries and tears, to him who was able to save him from death, and he was heard because of his reverence. Although he was a son, he learned obedience through what he suffered. And being made perfect, he became the source of eternal salvation to all who obey him, being designated by God a high priest after the order of Melchizedek (Heb. 5:7-10).

Even though it would be easy to view Gethsemane merely in the light of Christ's personal anguish as he faced the ordeal of Calvary, Hebrews makes it clear there was much more at stake. As Douglas Milne points out, this detail in the account of Christ's passion is integral to salvation.[3]

The second allusion to Christ at prayer that night comes later in the context of the author's encouragement to persevere with the eye of faith fixed firmly on Christ. He says,

> Consider him who endured from sinners such hostility against himself, so that you may not grow weary or faint-hearted. In your struggle against sin you have not yet resisted to the point of shedding your blood (Heb. 12:3, 4).

[3] D. J. W. Milne, *Let's Study Luke* (Edinburgh: Banner of Truth Trust, 2005), p. 343.

At first glance this may seem to point to Christ's shedding his blood through his death on the cross. The exhortation, therefore, being, 'Like Christ, stand firm against temptation, even to the point of death.' But a closer look at the wording would suggest the author actually has Gethsemane in view, since his choice of words in this exhortation contains echoes of Luke's account of Christ praying in the garden.

The first is his reference to 'your *struggle* [Greek: *antago-nizomenoi*] against sin' (echoing the Greek *en agonia*, Luke 22:44). The second is his choice of 'shedding your blood' as the measure of the intensity of this struggle. Although this could legitimately be understood as an exhortation to be 'faithful unto death,' if Jesus' ordeal in Gethsemane is indeed in the author's mind, then it more naturally reflects Jesus' utter commitment to his mission that would lead to the cross for its fulfilment. Again, this tallies with Luke's earlier reference to Jesus' resolve to go to Jerusalem (Luke 9:51) despite being aware of the suffering it would entail.

So, as Jesus not only urges the disciples to pray that they would not enter into temptation—'stumble in the conflict'—he also prays with eyes wide open to that looming conflict that he himself would not stumble. And such is the intensity of his struggle in prayer, that the Father provides him with an angel for support and 'his sweat became like great drops of blood falling down to the ground' (Luke 22:43, 44).

To understand what lay behind such intense internal conflict, we need to grasp something of the apparent paradox of his prayer: 'Father, if you are willing, remove this cup from me. Nevertheless, not my will, but yours, be done' (Luke 22:42). At face value, this would seem to suggest a conflict between the will of the incarnate Son and that of the Father. If that were the case, it would have major implications for the cohesion of the godhead. However, on deeper reflection, the reality is different. In the first place, this is because, in his request for the 'cup' (of judgment) to be taken from him, Jesus could have prayed no other way. As the eternal Son incarnate, from the moment of his conception he had fulfilled all righteousness and deserved only the Father's vindication, not judgment. Thus, just as he could pray no other way with his first request, so he could pray no other way with his second: 'Nevertheless, not my will, but yours, be done.' As the perfect man, whose delight it had been to do God's will and keep his law, he offered both these requests, knowing that the fulfilment of the divine will was essential for him to fulfil his saving mission.

The mystery of this salvation that comes from the God who is both just and yet justifies sinners is great. However, being allowed to look upon this mystery in the garden puts an altogether different complexion on it. We see its face: salvation is not just a concept, Jesus is its 'face.' We will never fully fathom what went on that night; but we will be able to sing the words of Charles H. Gabriel's great hymn:

> I stand amazed in the presence
> > Of Jesus the Nazarene
> And wonder how He could love me,
> > A sinner condemned, unclean!

How marvellous! how wonderful!
And my song shall ever be:
How marvellous! how wonderful!
Is my Saviour's love for me!

For me it was in the garden
  He prayed: 'Not My will, but Thine.'
He had no tears for His own griefs,
  But sweat drops of blood for mine.

In pity angels beheld Him,
  And came from the world of light
To comfort Him in the sorrows
  He bore for my soul that night.

He took my sins and my sorrows,
  He made them his very own,
He bore the burden to Calvary
  And suffered and died alone.

When with the ransomed in glory
  His face I at last shall see,
'Twill be my joy through the ages
  To sing of His love for me

10

Windows on the Crucifixion

I LOVE photography and, although I'm not a great photographer, I have learned some of the secrets of capturing a scene or portrait effectively. The most important of these is to choose angles that allow the details to stand out clearly. When it comes to understanding the cross of Christ, the Gospel writers employ a very similar principle. They all record the same event, but each provides his own distinctive perspective—John as an eyewitness, the Synoptic authors through the testimony of others. Together, their accounts provide us with the canonical history of what took place, each written in a way that allows the details to begin to interpret the event as a whole.

Even though the full exposition of this pivotal moment in the history of redemption is found in the Old Testament prelude to the event and the apostolic message of Acts, the Letters, and Revelation, the Gospels shed their own distinctive light on what Christ accomplished through the cross. In Luke's account of Calvary there are at least six distinctive angles that stand out from the accounts given by his fellow evangelists. Each provides a 'window' that sheds significant light on this, the darkest moment of history.

The first 'window' is on the state of our world (Luke 23:25-31). As Jesus sets out on that final journey along what is now called the *Via Dolorosa* towards the place of execution, Luke draws attention to details that are absent from the parallel accounts. Although he mentions Simon of Cyrene, it is almost in passing, and largely to acknowledge the extremity of Jesus' physical state by that time. Additionally, although he notes with the other Gospels that crowds gathered to watch this spectacle, Luke homes in on the significant numbers of women among them. In part, this tallies with the particular interest Luke has shown throughout his Gospel in the role of women in the ministry of Christ. But here it is not just their understandable grief and concern that becomes the focus; but, rather, what Jesus says to them. He tells them not to weep for him, but for themselves and their children (Luke 23:28-31). His last word to them comes in the form of a proverb: 'For if they do these things when the wood is green, what will happen when it is dry?' (Luke 23:31). If this is how humanity behaves when it is face to face with the incarnation of God's goodness in Christ, of what is it capable when the divine presence is withdrawn? Against all the protestations of the fundamental goodness of humanity today, the cross exposes the ugly truth about our world.

The second 'window' is on Christ's love for his enemies. Luke alone records Jesus' prayer from the cross: 'Father, forgive them, for they know not what they do' (Luke 23:34).

Commentators and theologians have argued over who the 'them' in the crowd that day might be, but there is no definitive answer. However, John Calvin offers a helpful observation:

> Christ gave evidence he was that mild and gentle lamb...for not only does he abstain from revenge, but pleads with God the Father for salvation of them by whom he was most cruelly tormented. He prays that God would forgive his enemies.[4]

Everything Jesus was doing that day was ultimately for those who were by nature and by choice the enemies of God.

The third 'window' Luke provides us with is on the glorious irony of the insults that were hurled against our Lord. He is not alone in drawing attention to them, but he does so in a way that shows a different aspect to them. Luke draws attention to three insults (Luke 23:35-38): the rulers' taunt, 'He saved others; let him save himself, if he is the Christ of God, his Chosen One!'; the soldiers' mockery, 'If you are the King of the Jews, save yourself!'; and the written charge, 'This is the King of the Jews.' It was not merely that they all stung uniquely because they contained words of truth; but because, if Jesus had chosen to save himself at that moment, then they would not have been true! Indeed, it could be argued for a variety of reasons that if Christ had chosen to abandon his God-given mission at that point, he would have stopped being God (if that were

---

[4] John Calvin, *Commentaries*, vol. 17 (Grand Rapids, MI: Baker, 1979), p. 300.

possible). Thus, in a perverse, but glorious way, the very insults inspired by Satan, the arch-mocker, were a declaration of the gospel itself.

The fourth 'window' Luke opens is on the breath-taking grace of salvation. Along with the other Gospel writers, Luke mentions the two criminals on either side of Christ; however, Luke alone records the conversion of one. At his conversion, the language Jesus uses to assure this man of his new state is among the sweetest found anywhere in Scripture: 'today you will be with me in paradise' (Luke 23:43). Even though they were nailed to death instruments that were synonymous with the divine anathema, they would end that day in the place of benediction. There really is no one too bad and it really never is too late to turn to Christ and find salvation.

The fifth 'window' is found in the signs that explain the cross (Luke 23:44-49). There were four in all, but Luke homes in on two: the darkness and the tearing of the curtain in the temple. These were not only signs from heaven designed to attest the divine significance of what was happening on earth, but were also intended to give a provisional explanation of what was happening. The darkness graphically demonstrated that God has ultimately dealt with the darkness of this age by his Son going to the very heart of its darkness on the cross. The fact the darkness lifted in the moments before Jesus' final cry, 'Father, into your hands I commit my spirit!' (Luke 23:46) and that all this coincided with the tearing of the curtain in the temple (Luke 23:45) sheds extraordinary light on what had been achieved. There is every reason to believe that the curtain in question was the heavy curtain barring access to the Most Holy Place for all people except for the high priest on the Day of Atonement. Thus, Jesus, 'the great high priest' who is 'after the order of Melchizedek' (Heb. 4:14; 5:10) had made atonement once-and-for-all in the place of his people and the way to God was now open through him.

Finally, there was Jesus' burial (Luke 23:50-56). Is this merely an incidental detail? Hardly, given that Paul includes it as one of those doctrines that is 'of first importance' (1 Cor. 15:3, 4), that he highlights its saving significance (Rom. 6:4), and that it is included as an article of faith in the *Apostles' Creed*. It is the glorious full stop to the record of the cross. The form of execution that embodied shame, humiliation, condemnation and curse was normally followed by the denial of burial for the corpses of the deceased. Often they would have been abandoned in a public place—the final symbol of disgrace, to decay under the elements and be eaten by carrion birds and animals. But it was not so for Jesus. He was formally and officially granted a burial with high honour. This was something the Jews would not have failed to notice. Despite the best efforts of the authorities to have him literally anathematised, he was laid to rest in a way that spoke of the divine favour at the very end.

One of the beauties of photographs is that they open windows on their subjects in a way that can be savoured. That's why we keep them in albums and display them in galleries. I wonder if there should not be some kind of Reformed resurrection of the Mediaeval practice of contemplation of the cross. For we can never appreciate it too much and there is far more to it than we will ever grasp.

II

No Longer Orphans

JESUS is simultaneously the master theologian and the perfect pastor. He sets the deepest of truths before his people, but in a way that pastorally meets their deepest needs. This should give pause for thought regardless of a person's relation to the church; it has something to say to theologians, pastors, Christians with no official role, and even to those who are not yet Christians.

It says something to theologians and those who love doctrine. The great truths God has revealed in his word are neither the preserve of the academy, nor the specialist. His truth is for all, and he has made it known in a way designed to bring wide-ranging benefit to all. It sharpens our understanding of God and of salvation, enhances worship, deepens trust, and encourages progress and perseverance in the faith. Grasping this will remind those who labour in the academy that they are ultimately the servants of the church—right down to the 'lambs of the flock' (cf. John 21:15).

It says something as well to pastors who do not see the connection between doctrine and pastoral care. Too often those who are pastor-teachers divide the functions bound up with their office. In the pulpit or classroom they are teachers, but in their role as shepherds, they are therapists who do not teach. If teaching is to be faithful to the Bible, it must have a pastoral dimension. Similarly, if pastoral care is to meet the deep needs of the God's flock, it must be deeply rooted in God's word. So the pulpit must always be pastorally informed and all pastoral care needs to be laced with God's life-transforming truth.

It also says something to Christians (and people who are not yet Christians) who are suspicious of doctrine—perhaps because they have only encountered it in language and forms that seem remote from their world. Just as a house needs strong foundations if it is to withstand the elements, so the household or house of faith needs a solid foundation to withstand the rigours of life. What we need is not more 'How to…' manuals for Christian living, we need a richer and deeper grasp of what it means to be a Christian.

We could quite literally dip in at random to any of Christ's didactic utterances on the one hand, or his pastoral involvement on the other, to see how all of this is worked out in his own ministry. One instance in particular has often struck me, not least because it immediately brings me back to the moment it first caught my attention when I was a small boy. That is the occasion in the upper room when Jesus—mid-flow in his initial explanation of the Holy Spirit's coming—said, 'I will not leave you as orphans; I will come to you' (John 14:18). There was something potent about Jesus' choice of words that captured my imagination.

At that time, books about orphaned children were fairly common so these words struck home with some force.

Of course, it has only been with the passage of time that the full weight of how Jesus chose to express himself to the disciples that night has begun to sink in more fully. This was potent language expressing potent truth, that in turn was to provide powerful comfort for these men who were beside themselves with fear. Their fears had been fuelled by Jesus' talk of his going away (John 13:33). It must have been hard enough over that final year of Christ's earthly ministry for them to cope with the growing opposition to their master, so it is understandable that the thought of his having to leave them was deeply troubling (John 14:1).

Jesus knew that a major factor in their unrest was a lack of knowledge. This was, in part, because they had yet to grasp the full depth and implications of what they had already been taught, but it was also because the climactic events of salvation history had yet to be revealed. However, his response to this lack was not to subject them to an intensive course in Biblical and Systematic Theology in the hours that remained.

The anchor points in the instruction Jesus gave that night were very personal. He consciously and deliberately reached for language and metaphor that touched their hearts in a way that would help engage their minds. At that moment, their minds were preoccupied with the fear, 'We're about to be all on our own!' 'Orphaned' may have flashed into their thoughts, or even been muttered under someone's breath, but Jesus anticipated this in his response. It is, however, the wider context of his response that gives it meaning and substance.

There was no way his little band of followers could have grasped or appreciated the full force of what Jesus was saying in that moment. He did not expect them to. Indeed, he openly said that it would only be in the future, after the Spirit had been given, that they would begin to see. Nevertheless, there was immediate comfort in those words that would temper the horrors they experienced in the three days that followed.

The depth of Jesus words at that moment would ultimately reveal the depth of hope bound up in the gospel of Christ in all its fullness. We see a clue in the way Jesus connects the coming of the Spirit with his own coming to them. He promises to send them 'another Helper, to be with you forever' (John 14:16). But then, after the promise that they will not be orphaned, he goes on to say in relation to the Spirit's coming, 'I will come to you' (John 14:18). The conundrum in this was, and is twofold, with difficulties being found in the connection between the gift of the Spirit and the coming of Christ on the one hand, and when it would become a reality on the other.

The answer to the relationship question is not confusion between the persons of the Trinity, but in the oneness and intimacy that exists between them. Christ's reference to 'another' *paracletos* (helper/advocate/counsellor) is to 'another of the same kind.' That is, as he had been his disciples' counsellor/comforter/strengthener and upheld them throughout his earthly ministry, so the Holy Spirit, who is of the same kind as he is, would do this for them. The same Holy Spirit who supported Jesus in his ministry would now support them, and he would not merely be sent by the Father (John 14:16), but by the Son as well (John 16:7). He is, as Paul would later say, 'the Spirit of Christ' (Rom. 8:9). Thus the Spirit, who is sent 'in my [i.e. Christ's] name' (John 14:26), brings Christ to his people in a way that is no longer limited by his physical incarnate presence on earth.

The answer to the 'when' question has been regarded by some as through the resurrection; but this fails to address the problem over the limits of Christ's physical presence on earth. It is better, as noted by Calvin and those who follow him, to see this in the link between Christ's ascension and Pentecost. Sinclair Ferguson summarises this well when he says, 'not only has Christ become one flesh with us in the incarnation, but following his ascension and our baptism with the Spirit, we become one Spirit with Christ, and, forsaking this world, we ascend to the life of the world to come more and more.'[5]

There could hardly be a deeper truth, yet nothing can compare with it in terms of the depth of comfort it provides for fearful Christians. In Christ, and by his Spirit, we really are 'no longer orphans.'

---

[5] Sinclair B. Ferguson, *Some Pastors and Teachers* (Edinburgh: Banner of Truth Trust, 2017), p. 131.

Section Three

The Church: God's Pilgrim People

As you come to him, a living stone rejected by men but in the sight of God chosen and precious, you yourselves like living stones are being built up as a spiritual house, to be a holy priesthood, to offer spiritual sacrifices acceptable to God through Jesus Christ. For it stands in Scripture:

'Behold, I am laying in Zion a stone,
    a cornerstone chosen and precious,
and whoever believes in him will not be put to shame.'

So the honour is for you who believe, but for those who do not believe,

'The stone that the builders rejected
    has become the cornerstone,'

and

'A stone of stumbling,
    and a rock of offence.'

They stumble because they disobey the word, as they were destined to do.

But you are a chosen race, a royal priesthood, a holy nation, a people for his own possession, that you may proclaim the excellencies of him who called you out of darkness into his marvellous light. Once you were not a people, but now you are God's people; once you had not received mercy, but now you have received mercy.

Beloved, I urge you as sojourners and exiles [NIV: aliens and strangers] to abstain from the passions of the flesh, which wage war against your soul. Keep your conduct among the Gentiles honourable, so that when they speak against you as evildoers, they may see your good deeds and glorify God on the day of visitation.

1 Peter 2:4-12

12

The One Holy, Catholic and Apostolic Church

CHRISTIANS have a remarkable ability to skew what the Bible teaches about the church. As with so many things in life, we tend to perceive and define it with ourselves as the key reference point. But when this happens it distorts both our understanding and our enjoyment of whatever is in view.

The most obvious way we do this is to see either our own church/denomination, or else the church we most admire as the benchmark for what we think it should be. Whether in terms of belief or practice, we find ourselves drawn to it because it matches what *we* are looking for. The flaw in this ought to be self-apparent, yet we stumble into it repeatedly. Our subjective judgement can never be the final arbiter of what is true and good.

It is not without significance that God's people through the ages have seen the need to objectify the truths taught in God's word, truths which never cease to challenge us. Regardless of how well we might think we know them, the core teachings of Scripture are so immense that we are constantly challenged to adjust our thinking in light of them. This comes out in a surprising way in the great catholic creeds of the church. Far from being minimalist summaries of Christian doctrine, they were designed to be maximalist expressions of truth in short compass. Brief and simple enough to be memorised, even by children, but sufficiently dense to consistently stretch even the most erudite theologian.

The *Apostles' Creed* captures the idea of the unity of the church tersely in its statement: 'I believe in the church, the communion of saints.' The *Nicene Creed*, however, says a lot more using the same number of words: 'I believe in one holy, catholic and apostolic church.' Whereas the statement enshrined in the *Apostles' Creed* most certainly has the church universal within its purview, it is expressed in a way that inclines its confessors to focus on its expression in denominations or local congregations. The issue, then, is whether the church is to be understood 'from the bottom up,' (as many groups making up a whole) or 'from the top down' (one whole containing many parts). The Nicene Fathers leave no doubt as to which is prior.

Why does this matter? For a multitude of reasons that are more relevant than ever to a post-Enlightenment generation that thinks instinctively 'from the bottom up.' Ours is the age that denies the very notion of 'metanarrative' or 'big picture.' 'Me and my world' loom so large in our thinking that we lose sight of the bigger factors that provide the larger context for our understanding. One does not have to look far to see how this impacts our generation's view of the church.

Grasping the Nicene formulation of the doctrine of the church will, in the first place, enable us to appreciate the church in the light of its essence. Paul points to this in relation to Christ's purpose in redemption being 'to purify for himself a people for his own possession' (Titus 2:14). In doing so he simply echoes what Jesus declared to his disciples at Caesarea Philippi: 'you are Peter, and on this rock I will build my church' (Matt. 16.18). This is Jesus' first recorded use of the word *ecclesia* (church) in his earthly ministry and it is significant that his focus is on the church universal and not on its local and regional expressions.

As Robert Letham helpfully argues, there must always be a logical as well as theological priority to the church universal having precedence over its other manifestations, organisationally as well as geographically. In terms of its very essence, its smaller and more localised expressions can only be understood in light of what it is in its totality.

In the second place, the Nicene formulation gives us a more meaningful appreciation of the church's unity and diversity. Despite its many facets, flavours and dimensions, the church is ultimately 'one,' and its oneness is defined by its being 'holy' (set apart for and wholly devoted to God). It is also 'catholic' (comprised of a rich diversity of churches/ congregations throughout history and throughout the world). And, for it to be the true church, it must be 'apostolic' (defined and governed by apostolic truth— which, by definition, rests upon its Old Testament foundation).

This has enormous pastoral relevance for churches in their self-understanding and also for their members in terms of how they regard 'other churches.' It delivers us from a parochial outlook on the body of Christ: struggling to see beyond the hedges and walls of our own particular expression of church. More than this, it fosters a genuine sense of joyful *koinonia* (fellowship), rejoicing with another part of the body when God blesses them, and showing them sympathy and support when suffering is their lot. The church really is bigger than we imagine and often God shocks us in the way he uses churches that do not align with our own particular grouping to advance the cause of Christ.

Lastly, this great creedal truth should be given a more functional role in the life of every church that dares to confess it. There is no place for our congregations to recite these words with fingers crossed behind our backs or mental caveats being inserted to restrict what *we* mean when we say them. These words bind us to the same 'devoted-to-God-passion-for-truth-with-large-hearted-catholicity' that has defined the very best and most orthodox expressions of the church throughout its history. When our churches recover this ancient vision for the church in all its fullness and glory, we will not only discover more of the beauty and joy of being part of the body of Christ, we will also become more effective in our efforts to reach the world with the gospel entrusted to us.

13

A Living, Loving and Legally Binding Relationship

THERE are many dimensions bound up with what it means to be a Christian and what is involved in belonging to the church. In its deepest sense it is all about the most glorious relationship any human being can have. Its roots stretch back into eternity past, its experience is bound up with our existential present, and its horizons take us into eternity future. It changes what we are in ourselves as we are united to Christ and, because of that same union; it will ultimately change what we shall be in the world to come, when God's saving work in us is brought to completion (Phil. 1:6).

However, our day-to-day experience of life in Christ can often be turbulent. We are never consistent in our efforts to live for God. Our faith is sometimes strong and sometimes weak. We stray, we stumble, and we sin. There are times when we doubt—even to the point of struggling over our assurance of faith and salvation. All this is part and parcel of normal Christian living. It was the experience of the patriarchs, prophets, and apostles, and it has continued to be the experience of genuine believers through the centuries. But we are not left to face this roller-coaster ride of faith alone.

From the very outset God has made it clear that his promised salvation is not something we experience in isolation. It is not a 'commodity' that becomes ours through some independent action. It is always only something that is found in and through relationship. Not merely relationship on the vertical plane between God and us as sinners, but a relationship that is reinforced on the horizontal plane through our being brought into God's family—fellow-believers who are there for our mutual support, encouragement, and loving admonition (when that is needed).

So, as we explore this mother lode of teaching on salvation that runs all the way through the Bible, we cannot help but be struck by how it is developed and viewed from many different angles. A key strand in this multifaceted doctrine is that of covenant—the binding relationship between God and man. Just as the fall, resulting in 'paradise lost,' was in essence the breach of relationship between God and man through Adam's disobedience, so salvation, 'paradise regained,' hinges on this relationship being restored.

The concept of 'covenant' is, in itself, rich with significance, and the Bible employs covenantal language in a range of ways. However, as we try to unpack what this language is intended to convey, it can be easy to emphasise one aspect of it at the expense of the other. For example, a great deal of interest in the theme of covenant has focused on the ancient Near Eastern suzerainty treaties of the Hittites and other ancient civilizations. These highlight the forensic elements of these nation-relationships and how they help us understand the forensic dimensions of relationship with God restored in redemption. However, the authors of Holy Scripture also reach for other expressions of covenant that were equally part of the cultures of their day and which—arguably to an even greater extent—provide a window into the one relationship that towers above all others. That is, the new relationship between God and his redeemed humanity.

The most common expression of 'covenant' that surfaces in the unfolding message of the Bible is not that of ancient suzerains and their vassal-states; but, rather, that of holy wedlock. The marriage covenant surfaces repeatedly as the Bible's preferred theological metaphor for the bond between God and his people. Two entire books in the Old Testament are built on the premise of marriage as it depicts how God and his people are bound together. Song of Solomon explores it positively, while Hosea does so negatively. Additionally, in the New Testament, the most exquisite portrayal of Christ and the church are expressed in terms of the unique relationship between a groom and his bride (Eph. 5:22-33; Rev. 19:1-9). The fact that Scripture makes us think of our saving bond with God in this way is meant to underscore that this gracious covenant is both a 'living and loving' as well as a 'legally binding' relationship.

Going back to the roller-coaster ride of the life of faith—at the church level as well as the individual level—it is a huge encouragement to see the double-lock built in to the divine guarantee enshrined in the gospel. Marriage for any husband and wife will, by degrees, be a roller-coaster ride of faith in each other, and with many marriages failing these days we may wonder about the security of this relationship. However, it is impossible for God to lie (Heb. 6:18) and he has promised an everlasting marriage, 'I will betroth you to me forever. I will betroth you to me in righteousness and in justice, in steadfast love and in mercy. I will betroth you to me in faithfulness. And you shall know the LORD' (Hos. 2:19, 20).

Interestingly, this doctrine of the unity of the church surfaces from a different angle, but still from within the perspective of family, in the prologue to John's Gospel. There, having announced the coming of Christ into the world and declaring that the world did not recognise him and that his own people—the Jews—did not receive him (John 1:10, 11), John goes on to spell out what happens to those who do receive him by faith. He says, 'But to all who did receive him, who believed in his name, he gave the right to become children of God, who were born, not of blood nor of the will of the flesh nor of the will of man, but of God' (John 1:12, 13). In many ways the language employed by the apostle takes us beyond what is conveyed by the use of marriage as an image of restored relationship. It takes the idea of 'living and loving, and legally binding' to a whole new level.

John is speaking about the new life found in Christ in terms of adoption: to them 'he gave the *right* to become the children of God.' This is a legal entitlement, underwritten by the supreme court of heaven itself. It is inviolable—even by our most tragic failures as God's adopted ones. The rights conferred cannot be revoked, because they are sealed in the Son of God, Jesus. Not only this, but our legal standing as Christians in this relationship is underpinned by something more: the living bond into which we are brought through regeneration. We are born again/from above through the Spirit of God. The death that was ours by nature has been exchanged for the life of God through his Spirit in union with his Son.

Human beings are complex creatures. We are multi-layered and multi-faceted. But God in his grace has taken all those complexities into consideration as he has crafted the great salvation provided through his Son. So, as we ride out the ups and downs of the Christian life, it is profoundly comforting to know we are 'strapped in' to our saving union with God through Christ by these two strands of our covenantal bond: legal, the right to be God's children; and experiential, the living bond into which we are brought.

14

The Church in All Her Glory

In the Western world at least, the glory of the church seems to be fading fast. Far from those days when her influence was far-reaching and wide-ranging, her values and opinions respected and her numbers strong; she has become the object of public ridicule and, too often, seen as the great irrelevance. Therefore, it is, perhaps, not surprising that Christians and even Christian ministers are tempted to keep their church affiliation and involvement to themselves. These are challenging times for many churches.

The answer to such discouragement is not simply to seek solace in the fact the church is thriving in many other parts of the world—even in surprising regions like China and parts of the Middle East—but to look at Scripture. In Scripture, we not only find a theology of church, but we also find its history; there it is traced from its earliest beginnings in the garden of Eden with its portrait painted, in Cromwell's words, 'warts and all.'

As we follow the unfolding history of the church and explore the details of how it is portrayed—in its worst seasons, as well as the best—we discover the kind of insights and doctrinal markers that give us a true perspective on this body to which we belong. Surprisingly, it is often in unexpected places that we find the greatest encouragement.

This is especially true when we explore the church of Israel in some of her darkest times in the Old Testament. There were certainly chapters in the history of the church under its old covenant administration when its future seemed very bleak. The days of the judges were an obvious example of this, as too were the four hundred-year 'Dark Ages' between the Testaments. But even in the darkest times, the lights never went out. In keeping with God's promise to Abraham, his determination to bless the nations through the blessings of salvation he bestowed on Israel would not be thwarted.

Some of the most encouraging insights into the nature and destiny of the church found anywhere in the Bible emerge from the prophecy of Isaiah. He, like the other major prophets, was called to serve in some of the most difficult times God's ancient people ever went through. It was the era of the two-stage disintegration of the Northern and Southern Kingdoms, culminating in the permanent diaspora for the North, and the seventy-year exile of the South. Even when the restoration of the Southern Kingdom took place under Ezra and Nehemiah, the Southern Kingdom never regained its former glory, stability or spiritual strength.

It would be tempting, therefore, to think that God's message through these great preacher-theologians would have been one of unremitting condemnation. However, although this is partially true—Isaiah especially has great swathes that are filled with foreboding—the weight of grace and gospel interwoven into them is quite extraordinary. Indeed, it is, perhaps, especially because these glimpses of salvation are set against some of the darkest backdrops found anywhere in Scripture that they stand out so brightly.

There are many examples of this, but one stands out especially. It is found in Isaiah 60, and is striking because it comes hard on the heels of two entire chapters in which God confronts his people with a catalogue of their sins and failures and reminds them of what they deserve. Yet, even though they are not completely devoid of hope, it would have been despair that loomed largest on the horizon for their original audience.

If there seemed to be anything for these people to cling on to in the face of God's words to them in that section, it would perhaps have been the idea of 'a remnant'—scrap of cloth hanging on by a thread—that God said would survive. But God had far more in mind for them in terms of where their future lay. Theirs would be a future that would stretch far beyond their wildest expectations, a future bound up with the greatest glory imaginable.

Astonishingly, this had to do with the church's witness to the world (Isa. 60:1-3). These people, who in the previous chapter had said, 'we hope for light, and behold, darkness, and for brightness, but we walk in gloom' (Isa. 59:9), were now being told, 'Arise, shine, for your light has come, and the glory of the LORD has risen upon you.' However, it was more than just this. Not only would God's light in all its glory shine on them, but through them it would light up the world to the extent that, 'nations shall come to your light, and kings to the brightness of your rising.'

The dawning of this new day came when Jesus, 'the light of the world' (John 8:12) came into the world and, through him, his people become the light of the world in a derivative sense (Matt. 5:14-16). The full force of this began to become apparent on the Day of Pentecost, when people who had come to Jerusalem from the nations heard the gospel and brought home the light that came from another world. The aftershocks of Pentecost continue to reverberate through the ages and across the world today.

The prophet builds on his remarkable statement with something even more remarkable: the fact that the church would ultimately become a home for all nations (Isa. 60:8-14). Once again, this seemed to beggar belief for the faithful few Isaiah was addressing. They instinctively thought the opposite. They were about to be torn from their homes and homeland and deported to places where they could never feel 'at home.' But God informed them differently. He spoke of just how far the influence of the church would reach: to distant places—some named, others not— and to the fact that even their kings would make their way through the gates of God's new community (Isa. 60:8-13). The survey God gave was of the whole known world of that time. However, God's community has become a sanctuary for the entire cross-section of humanity in all its classes as much as for the spread of its ethnic groupings. Once more, the fulfilment of these words is seen from the earliest days of the church's expansion in Acts and has been charted through the history of the church ever since.

Everything Isaiah is saying in this surprising chapter ultimately points to the church as the pride and joy of God's people through all generations to come (Isa. 60:15-22). Despite their beleaguered state at the time the words were first spoken, the future would tell a different story. God says, 'Whereas you have been forsaken and hated, with no one passing through, I will make you majestic for ever, a joy from age to age' (Isa. 60:15). The reason for this is not because of what the church could ever be in itself, but only through what it has become in union and communion with Christ, God's promised redeemer. The church is loved by God and that love has been displayed most dramatically in the price he has paid to make it his very own. Indeed, even here in one of the church's darkest hours, God gives his people a glimpse of the heaven we see at the very end of Revelation where there is no need of sun or moon because God himself will be their light (Isa. 60:19-20). Even when his people are at their very worst, God will not let them lose sight of the very best he has secured for their eternal future.

Isaiah's words resonate with the church of our day because they tally with our own sense of coldness and failure—certainly in many parts of the West. But they also resonate with us because of the comfort they bring when we are tempted to lose heart. The key is not to introspect, but, following where the prophet's finger points, to look out and up to the saviour-king in whom our future is secure. He is our glory and often he chooses to shine most brightly in the darkest times.

15

'She Is His New Creation'

THERE is a popular notion that the Christian church originated from a decision by a handful of followers of Jesus
of Nazareth to start a movement. In the same way as other
world religions started and grew through human determination and effort, it is often assumed that the Christian
church is just a hugely successful example of the same thing.
However, the Bible tells us otherwise. It is both interesting
and significant that Paul reaches for the language of divine
creation to help his readers in Corinth grasp what the
church actually is. He describes it as his 'new creation,' and
his choice of words point to the ultimate new beginning
(2 Cor. 5:17).

The church in Corinth was arguably one of the most
confused and compromised of all the churches mentioned
in the New Testament. Yet it is to that church and the people
who belonged to it that Paul speaks about their being part
of God's new creation by virtue of their being 'in Christ.'

Many English translations manage to miss the full impact
of this verse by translating it, 'if anyone is in Christ, he is
a new creation' with the emphasis being on what they are

individually. Paul's horizon is set much higher. The letter actually reads, 'If anyone is in Christ, new creation!' Paul wants his readers to realise their salvation is much bigger than a mere private and personal experience. Every time someone is joined to the Lord Jesus Christ through new birth, he or she is not only incorporated into the life of Christ, but into what one theologian[1] colourfully calls 'that bundle of life' which all his people share in their union with him.

Different New Testament writers refer to this one reality using different word-pictures. John uses the language of new birth that Jesus used with Nicodemus (John 3:3-8). Elsewhere, Paul describes it in terms of Christians having been raised up together with Christ (Eph. 2:4-6; Rom. 6:5). Here, he uses the language of 'new creation.' Of course, they are more than just great images; they are great realities. The 'birth from above' Christians receive from the Holy Spirit is new life from God. The resurrection to a whole new life we are promised is as real as the resurrection life of Jesus himself. So too the new creation of which Paul speaks is every bit as real as the creation God brought into being in Genesis and what it will become when Jesus comes again to usher in perfection (Rev. 21:5). Samuel Stone expressed it eloquently in his hymn about the church with the lines,

> The church's one foundation
> Is Jesus Christ her Lord;
> She is His new creation
> By water and the word.

---

[1] Sinclair B. Ferguson, echoing Thomas Goodwin.

It is impossible to overstate the deep significance of what Paul says here about Christ and his relationship with the church. The whole idea of being part of this new creation is intimately bound up with a person's being 'in Christ.' But there is more to it as well. It is, as we have already pointed out, what we are and ultimately will be corporately as his redeemed people that displays the whole new order of existence to which we now belong. In Christ we have been given a new heart (Ezek. 36:26), a new mind (Rom. 12:1-2) and a whole new orientation in life (Eph. 4:17). Most significantly, we have been given a whole new future as well. Even though as members of the church we live in this world, we actually belong to another world—God's world. As Paul tells the Christians in the Roman colony of Philippi, even though they and he were Roman citizens, because of their relationship with Christ, 'our citizenship is in heaven' (Phil. 3:20). The full expression of what 'heaven' is will only become clear when Jesus Christ returns and ushers in God's new creation in its full and final perfection—'a new heaven and a new earth' (Rev. 21:1).

Just as the race God made to bear his image was the centrepiece of his original creation, so—not surprisingly— his redeemed and renewed race will be the centrepiece of his new creation. The 'holy city, new Jerusalem…prepared as a bride, adorned for her husband' of which John speaks (Rev. 21:2) is a vivid metaphor for a redeemed humanity. It is vital to realise that this new community does not exist in some kind of ethereal vacuum, but belongs to the renewed 'natural habitat' God intended for our race. It will be in a renovated world and universe which has been set free from God's curse (Rom. 8:19-21), and it will become part of the 'new world' (Matt. 19:28) that Jesus says will come to be when he comes again.

When we begin to appreciate the church as God's new creation, it helps us grasp where it fits into the grand scheme of things in terms of what has gone wrong in our world, what Christ has done to put things right, and where it ultimately will lead when God's saving purpose is complete.

16

The Indispensable Mark of the Church

'WHAT are the marks of a true church?' is a question that has quite rightly occupied the minds of theologians through the centuries, because the history of the church is littered with many bodies that have claimed to be churches, but have drifted so far from their moorings in Scripture that they are no longer genuine. But what marks should we be looking for to identify a church that is both true and faithful?

We might be forgiven for instinctively reaching for the answer that has been widely embraced by Reformed and evangelical churches through the ages. Namely, a church that faithfully preaches and teaches the word of God, faithfully administers the sacraments and is faithful in maintaining discipline in the church. These three identifiers—or some permutation of them—were highlighted in the Reformation and post-Reformation eras in response to the Roman Catholic view that true churches should be recognised through their allegiance to the Pope.

It is interesting to note, however, that although the Bible places a very clear premium on all three of these vital signs of fidelity and orthodoxy, it places one other mark above them all. Indeed, it is the only mark of a genuine church that is formally identified and the one who draws the church's attention to it is none other than Jesus himself. He told the disciples—who were on the brink of becoming the foundation stones of the New Testament church—'By this all people will know that you are my disciples, if you have love for one another' (John 13:35). In making this statement Jesus was by no means suggesting that faithfulness to his word, the sacraments or to a disciplined approach to church life did not matter. Rather, he meant that the one quality that must suffuse all three (and indeed church life generally) is love.

We see the importance of this worked out in the real-life pastoral crisis facing the church in Corinth some thirty years after Jesus spoke these words. The church had been founded relatively recently under the ministry of Paul, but within a very short space of time had gotten into serious difficulties. It had begun to embrace teachings that were in conflict with the Bible—especially in relation to Christ's teaching on the resurrection. Its administration of the sacraments, notably the Lord's Supper, had become a mark of disgrace for the church. Even though there had been serious moral and spiritual failure in the church, if it had not been for Paul's intervention, there would have been no meaningful attempt from within the church to deal with them. Yet, interestingly, despite such significant failures in relation to all three marks of the church, the apostle did not declare it apostate. Indeed, it would appear from the other evidence we have[2] that Paul

[2] From 2 Corinthians and his reference to another letter he wrote which no longer exists.

invested considerable time and effort in seeking to restore the situation there.

The most striking thing of all in the way Paul addresses the situation is in what he has to say about the role of love in the restoration of this failing church. In a very real sense, he makes it clear that love is the one mark of an authentic church that is indispensable. Even when a congregation such as this one may have stumbled so badly in its conduct, drifted seriously in its handling of Scripture and so misused the sacraments to have bordered on the scandalous, the presence (or lack) of love among its people will be the key to seeing where it really stands and where it will finally end up.

When Paul speaks in depth about this necessary characteristic of the church in 1 Corinthians 13, some people regard it as a digression because it appears to break the flow about church life and church worship that forms the focus of attention in the chapters on either side. But to see it as some kind of interruption to his train of thought would be to miss the point of what Paul is doing. As the apostle uses this discourse on love to touch on every issue he has already addressed and will go on to address, he is showing his readers there is one element in solving these issues that is common to them all: the need for love. However, what is perhaps most striking of all is what the apostle says about where this love ultimately leads.

In the closing section of the chapter he speaks about things that had a vital part to play in the life and growth of the church in the New Testament era—namely, prophecies, tongues, and knowledge—but all of them will 'pass away'

(1 Cor. 13:8). Those things that loomed large—too large on the horizons of this church—will not last. In contrast, love will last. It alone will never fail. He goes on, in the remainder of the chapter, to impress three important things on his listeners.

The first is that love outlives all other things that matter. Paul points to what will happen when 'the perfect comes' (1 Cor. 13:10). The word translated 'perfect' conveys the sense of endpoint, completeness, fulfilment, or maturity. Given that the section begins with Paul saying 'love never fails' (1 Cor. 13:8) and ends with, 'So now faith, hope, and love abide, these three; but the greatest of these is love' (1 Cor. 13:13), it is hard not to see the link Paul is making between the supremacy of love when it comes into its own and the 'perfection' of which he has been speaking. If we take the arrival of this perfection to be with the second coming of Christ (as many commentators do), then it only serves to heighten the church's appreciation of love in the here and now.

How might we translate this into the post-New Testament era in which we live? Revelation, along with its proclamation and understanding, are all vital to church life in this age, but none is an end in itself. They point us and lead us to the perfection that is to come, and love is the key to how they get us there. Love takes us from the means by which God is pleased to make himself known—the word written, proclaimed, and received by faith—to the redeemed relationships with himself and with each other for which those means were given.

In the second place, love is the measure of our maturity in the life of faith. Just as all human expressions of love mature in the course of natural development, the same is true when it comes to our spiritual growth and development. In a not-so-subtle way, Paul prods the Corinthians over their childish behaviour and failure to grow up in the faith as they were taught from the word. For that reason, he reminds them how the limitations of Christian experience in the here and now will inevitably be eclipsed by the church's 'coming of age' in the world to come (1 Cor. 13:11, 12). In that sense, learning to love God as the revealer and the giver (rather than his revelation and the gifts in themselves) becomes the measure of our progress towards maturity in the faith.

The last point Paul makes is to show that love, in a unique sense, endures from this world to the next. The closing verse speaks of three vital components of Christian experience that remain (in time), but one stands out as being 'the greatest' because it will outlive time. Faith is vital, but it must give way to sight. Hope is crucial, but one day it must become reality. Only love will last, and it will ultimately come into its own in the perfection of the new heavens and the new earth. Only there and only then will we know and love as we have been known and loved by God—and this will transform both our interpersonal relationships and our relationship with God.

In a very real sense, then, love becomes the link between this world and the next. The arms of love that pulled us out of the mire of our lostness and carried us through the life of faith in this fallen world will carry us finally into that coming age. The God who 'is love,' is himself that link through Jesus Christ our loving Lord and saviour, by the Holy Spirit, through whom he sheds his love in the hearts of all his people.

17

Discipline: A Misconstrued Grace

IT was John Knox, the Scottish Reformer, who added discipline to the word and sacraments as the third mark of a faithful church. In doing so he rightly highlighted the need for this third element of church life for the church to be what it ought to be under Christ, its sole king and head. Sadly, however, discipline has too often been misperceived as some kind of blunt instrument only to be used as a measure of last resort when things go wrong in the church. However, it is utterly wrong to see it only in these terms. John Knox certainly did not see it narrowly in that way and neither do the Scriptures.

Knox's *Book[s] of Discipline* were drawn up as books of church order. They were intended to be the practical outworking of the doctrine summarised in the *Scots Confession*. Since doctrine is always intended to shape life, so the Reformer wisely saw fit to spell this out under specific headings as it related to the life and worship of the church. The Westminster Divines did something very similar over eighty years later when they drew up the *Directory for Public Worship* and the *Form of Church Government*. Both these documents put practical flesh on the doctrinal bones of what the church was taught to confess.

These aspects of 'discipline' are a healthy counterbalance to the narrow view of its use as an extreme last resort. They remind us that, just as with our natural human families, the church needs to be a well-ordered community as the family of God. What is more, the order to which it conforms must be that ordained by God himself in his triune wisdom and glory.

Scripture provides a further insight into what discipline entails and how God uses it for the good of his children. We see this towards the end of Hebrews, where the writer is speaking of the means God uses to enable his people to go the distance in the life of faith: persevering to the very end. Immediately after his exhortation to run with perseverance the race that is set before us with our eyes firmly fixed on Jesus (Heb. 12:1, 2), the writer goes on to say, 'My son, do not regard lightly the discipline of the Lord, nor be weary when reproved by him. For the Lord disciplines the one he loves, and chastises every son whom he receives' (Heb. 12:5, 6).

In the context of the letter the writer clearly had something in view that was more than just the church being ordered under God by its leaders, or their having to exercise formal 'church discipline' in the face of the threatened apostasy by some of its members. He speaks of 'hardship' as 'discipline' (Heb. 12:7)—almost certainly a reference to the harsh providences these believers had recently experienced. It seems likely that these Hebrew believers belonged to the church in Rome and had suffered significantly under persecution—right down to numbers of them being martyred for the faith. Hence the writer's words were designed to help them see God's hand at work even in such painful experiences.

This tallies with what the Scriptures say elsewhere about how God uses suffering to strengthen character, burn off the spiritual dross in our lives and teach us perseverance in the faith. In that sense, as Peter tells his readers, we should not be surprised by it, or regard it as 'something strange' (1 Pet. 4:12).

There is, however, something very distinctive about the Hebrews statement on discipline. It places it firmly in the context of God's dealing with his people as 'sons' (an expression that includes women as well as men to signify that both share the same status and privilege in God's family) and proof that they are not in fact 'illegitimate children.' Despite its potentially negative feel, it is intended to have a manifestly positive function. Rather than wearing us down in the faith, it is intended to build us up.

This makes perfect sense in the competitive world we live in. In this world people push themselves, whether it be in the realm of sport with its personal trainers and rigorous fitness regimes, or that of academia or commerce where people routinely push themselves to be the best they can be. Why should we be surprised at the thought of God's pushing us beyond our slothful limits to build us up? If people in the world around us accept hardship as a means of improving fitness, character, personal well-being, and effectiveness; how much more should this be true for Christians as they accept the disciplines of God's family in all their many forms. In this sense, 'discipline' should be a most glorious component of church life and very much part of the experience of every Christian. It should not be seen as a 'stick in the cupboard' for the erring few; but another aspect of the grace of God.

18

The Great Neglected Mandate

LAST words are important and often intriguing and none more so than the last words of Jesus. They are best remembered as expressed by Matthew at the end of his Gospel where Jesus tells the eleven,

> All authority in heaven and on earth has been given to me. Go therefore and make disciples of all nations, baptizing them in the name of the Father and of the Son and of the Holy Spirit, teaching them to observe all that I have commanded you. And behold, I am with you always, to the end of the age (Matt. 28:18-20).

They are familiar words and, even though they are almost certainly not Jesus' last words in a chronological sense, they linger in a way those recorded at the start of Acts do not. These 'last words' the disciples heard from Christ would galvanise the significance of the first words he spoke to them (as recorded by Matthew) in a way that would change them forever. Their formal relationship with Christ began with the words, 'Follow me, and I will make you fishers of men' (Matt. 4:19). Now that relationship came of age, as he prepared to leave them, saying, 'Go…!'

There are numerous angles from which we can view this parting mandate from Christ, but one that is perhaps not often considered is its relationship to another mandate found at another defining moment in the history of the world and of the human race. That is, the so-called 'Creation Mandate' recorded at the end of the opening chapter of Genesis.

Immediately after the description of God's creation of humanity God says to them, 'Be fruitful and multiply and fill the earth and subdue it and have dominion over the fish of the sea and over the birds of the heavens and over every living thing that moves on the earth' (Gen. 1:28).

As Greg Beale points out, the fact that this command is introduced with words that relate to procreation provides a significant link between God's words in Eden and his words through the risen Christ on the Mount of Olives.

The clue to the connection lies in the context of creation. In the newly established creation in Genesis, crowned with the first pair of human beings as God's image-bearers, God commands Adam and Eve to replicate and perpetuate that image throughout the earth. On the Mount of Olives, we encounter Christ as the prototypical man who, through his resurrection from the dead, has inaugurated God's new creation. So, there should be no surprise at his speaking words that echo those spoken to the first Adam in his perfection. Those who, in Christ, are 'new creation' (2 Cor. 5:17) are also to replicate and perpetuate the restored image through their gospel witness and labours.

Within the context of the New Covenant community, this clearly had implications for the families of believers and how they were to be nurtured in the faith (Acts 2:39; Eph. 6:1-4). However, in this fallen world it had a larger horizon as well. They were to 'make disciples of all nations'—nations, which at that time, were very much outside the covenant community of the people of God. The mandate is now to be outworked in a fallen world among the countless millions in whom the image of God—often called by the Latin, *imago dei*—(Gen. 1:26, 27) is disfigured. How is the church to fulfil this task? By bearing witness to the only one in and through whom the image can be savingly restored, namely Jesus (Acts 1:8). The apostolic witness entrusted to the church finds its gospel focus in Christ alone as saviour.

The precise wording of the Great Commission is significant. Even though, at least for those who only read it in an English translation, it would be tempting to think the 'command' component of what Jesus says is to 'Go!', the imperative in this clause is actually to 'make disciples.' The 'going' is presented as a participle before the imperative. This usually indicates action prior to the main verb and so this suggests that Jesus assumes we need to be going in order to make disciples: we might say the church needs to be in a 'going mode' as it brings the gospel to the world.

Sadly, the church has repeatedly distorted Christ's words at this point by understanding them to mean, 'Come and hear!' (supposedly addressed to the world). But, of course, our Lord addressed his command to the embryonic New Testament church that they should 'Go and tell!'

The salient difference between what is said in this context and its Old Testament precursors in Israel's calling to be a light to the Gentiles and God's means of bringing all nations to praise him (see, e.g. Psa. 67:1-7) is that now, through the death and resurrection of Christ, salvation had been fully accomplished. This is why Jesus can emphatically preface his word of command with a word of promise: 'All authority in heaven and on earth has been given to me. Go therefore…' (Matt. 28:18, 19). More than that, it explains why he can also punctuate the commission with the assurance, 'And behold, I am with you always, to the end of the age' (Matt. 28:20).

Christians in the increasingly post-Christian Western world wring their hands in face of declining church attendance and ever-growing opposition to God and the gospel. Yet, strangely, as the gospel is spreading and the church is rapidly growing in the Majority world, it is invariably in the face of even greater opposition: ignorance, world religions, and persecution. This was very much the world into which Jesus was thrusting the apostolic band through his last word to them. Their mission 'to the Jew first and also to the Greek [referring to all non-Jews]' (Rom. 1:16) seemed like an impossible task; but as these men gave themselves to it in faith and obedience, Christ used them to begin building his church. That is what he has been doing ever since as his people everywhere dare to risk their all for the gospel.

19

Diversity Is Not Optional

'DIVERSITY' has become one of the buzzwords in evangelical Christianity in recent times. At one level, this is a good thing, but at another, its trendy inclusion may come at an unwelcome price. Just as a perfectly good adjective like 'missional' became a cover for some less than good theology, we can only hope the word 'diversity' does not become an umbrella word for a sociological rather than a theological agenda.

That said, it is not that long since the idea of diversity was regarded with suspicion in many church circles. This was true largely for cultural reasons. Consciously or otherwise, the church has done throughout its history what it was seen to do in biblical times: namely, sanctify the cultural prejudices of its day to make room for them in the church. When people have come to faith, they have often had the sad habit of not leaving their cultural baggage at the door. But sadder still is that too often the church has not taught them otherwise.

Whether it has been on the basis of class or ethnicity, academic ability or social network, the fault-lines that divide the church in its broader expression are often just a reflection of the way society is congenitally divided. The upshot of this has been churches that are mono-ethnic and mono-cultural which allow no room for those perceived as outsiders to be welcomed.

In the days of Jesus, that prejudice was seen in the disciples proud boast that they had stopped a man driving out demons in Christ's name because 'he was not following us' (Mark 9:38). It did not matter that he had been using the Master's name and authority to exercise this ministry, he was outside their accepted group and, therefore, was denied the right to be part of their work. However, the disciples' rebuke led only to their being rebuked by Jesus himself as he told them not to hinder such people.

The issue took on a larger scale early on in New Testament church history. The need to choose the first seven men for diaconal roles in the church arose because of conflict between believing Jews from a Hebraic background and those from a Hellenistic background. Despite their shared spiritual background, their cultural differences had led to conflict and a refusal to work for the common good within the church.

By the time Paul was writing to the Galatians—possibly as early as AD 48—the issue was starting to become a crisis for New Testament Christianity. Indeed, it most likely had already become the main issue that most threatened the peace and unity of the embryonic New Testament church. It was certainly the catalyst for calling the first General Assembly of the church—the Jerusalem Council—recorded in Acts 15. Christians from a Jewish background were making the rites and regulations of Mosaic Law a condition for believers from a Gentile background being accepted as part of the church. As a result, the church generally, and individual congregations in particular, were being divided along social, religious, and ethnic lines, causing deep rifts in the body of Christ.

Paul addresses the issue forcibly (and at times aggressively) in his letter to the Galatians. But he does so from a different perspective in Ephesians—especially in the first three chapters. The whole thrust of the Ephesian letter is to show how the gospel impacts us as community. In the language of John Stott, it displays 'God's new community.'

In that context, the apostle makes a quite remarkable statement about God's grand design for the church:

> …so that through the church the manifold wisdom of God might now be made known to the rulers and authorities in the heavenly places. This was according to the eternal purpose that he has realized in Christ Jesus our Lord (Eph. 3:10, 11).

The word translated 'manifold' could more literally be rendered, 'multi-coloured'. In other words, in essence what he is saying is the church is the stage on which God has seen fit to display his multi-coloured wisdom to the watching world and universe.

We need to see the wider context of this statement. In particular, we need to see what Paul has said in the preceding chapter about Christ's having 'broken down in his flesh the dividing wall of hostility' (Eph. 2:14) between

Jew and Gentile through the cross. The multi-coloured character of God's wisdom is displayed in the literally multi-coloured—multi-ethnic—character of the church. So precious is this gift of salvation that unites an erstwhile fragmented humanity, that Paul tells the church to be 'eager to maintain the unity of the Spirit in the bond of peace' (Eph. 4:3). Diversity in the church was not an optional extra that the Ephesian Christians were free to take or leave at their pleasure.

It is not hard to see the relevance of this strand of teaching to many churches today. Ever since Donald McGavran began writing on church growth, advocating the principle of the 'homogeneous church unit,' a subtle but dangerous departure from biblical truth began to be canonized in evangelical circles. Non-diversity was no longer an accident of culture that churches quietly took on board; rather, it was something actively promoted as a key to growing churches. McGavran's ideology has gained further endorsement more recently from several key leaders in the Reformed church growth movement as they proactively promote the notion that we need to target specific sectors of the community to plant churches that are customized to suit their tastes.

If we take seriously not only the teaching of Paul (and the sectarian failures of Peter for which he was rebuked), nothing could be further from the truth. Diversity is not an option; it is a necessity. Indeed, if the gospel really is 'the power of God for salvation' (Rom. 1:16), then a church that is reaching out with that gospel in its community should expect to see the cross-section of its local community reflected in its membership.

Just as God himself is not a homogeneous unit, so those who bear his image as his redeemed community on earth should reflect the glory of his being as well as his character here on earth—in all its glorious diversity!

20

Keeping Churches Safe and Sound

CHURCHES (as communities of professing Christians) are meant to be safe places. Unfortunately, all too often, this has not been the case. Revelations of widespread abuse in many churches has seriously damaged the reputation and trustworthiness of the church as a whole before the watching world.

It could be rightly argued, however, that the violation of the church's safety in recent times is related to an even greater violation that goes back much further than the incidents being reported by the media. That is, the violation of its commitment to preserving sound teaching from the Bible. Both Old and New Testaments declare repeatedly that when the church departs from sound doctrine, it inevitably leads to corrupt behaviour.

This is very much the concern of the Apostle John in the three New Testament letters that bear his name. He was, by this time, an old man—possibly in his eighties—and according to church tradition, he had left Jerusalem in the aftermath of the city's overthrow in the 70s AD and was now resident in Ephesus. From there he exercised a ministry of pastoral care and instruction for the churches of that region.

The two big issues that dominated his concern for them were the false teaching rampant in those churches (causing significant division in some) and the unchristian conduct to which it was linked.

Although they tend to be lost in the shadow of his first letter, 2 and 3 John actually have a great deal to say to both these issues, but from a very pastoral perspective. 2 John was addressed to 'the chosen lady and her children' (2 John 1)—almost certainly veiled language for a local church and its members—and 3 John to 'Gaius' who may well have been an Elder in that same church. Both allow us an up close and personal glimpse of the best kind of pastoral care in action. In the case of 2 John, the apostle is concerned to address what is needed to keep churches 'safe and [doctrinally] sound,' while 3 John spells out what is involved in safeguarding faithful ministry in the church. I take up the first of these concerns here.

Several things stand out in what John said to encourage this church in the struggles it was facing, but they all crystallise in his exhortation to 'abide in the teaching of Christ' (2 John 9).

The first thing that stands out is the way he encourages these believers to keep going in their struggle and not lose heart. The apostle's choice of words in his salutation and greeting is deliberately crafted so as to lift their spirits and remind them they are not alone in what they are facing. He makes it clear in the opening verse that the sentiments expressed in what follows are not only his, but are shared by churches everywhere that are loyal to the truth revealed in Scripture. Regardless of how they may have been feeling in the thick of their troubles, John was giving the strongest assurance God's promise would not fail. Whatever its cost, their struggle to be faithful was not in vain.

Secondly, he reminds his readers about the link between law and love in the way God relates to his people and how he equips them to live for him in this world. This is one of the keynote truths John has woven deeply through the teaching in his first letter. In his writing, he echoes what Jesus himself taught his disciples in the Upper Room: 'If anyone loves me, he will keep my word' (John 14:23). He stresses this truth because the impact of false teaching on the churches at that time was leading to blatant disobedience on the part of many who claimed to love Jesus (2 John 7). John makes it clear that the connection between love and obedience is crucial. He rejoices that those to whom he was writing know this already and have not wavered in their commitment to it (2 John 4), but he urges them to keep on going. It is a principle that every church needs to know and implement in its life corporately if it is to remain 'safe' for those who seek refuge among its people.

Interestingly, the third angle John provides on this issue shows how this dual devotion to sound teaching and faithful living is not only bound up with God's glory, but also with the eternal good of his people. Once again, he points the finger at the false teachers who had infiltrated so many churches at that time, denying fundamental gospel truths—not least those which relate to the nature of the incarnation of Christ. He denounces them as 'antichrist' (2 John 7). But he then turns back to his faithful listeners, urging them 'not to lose' what they 'have worked for' in order that they 'may win a full reward' (2 John 8). That is, that they may remain faithful to the gospel message that not only brought them to faith in Christ, but also had thus far been building them up in fellowship with him and one another, and which alone will bring them home to glory. In so doing, he warns against anyone who 'goes on ahead and does not abide in the teaching of Christ,' because such a person 'does not have God' (2 John 9).

The issue at stake was of such seriousness that John tells his readers, in the fourth place, that if anyone came to their church teaching a faulty Christology, he should not be welcomed or given any hospitality (2 John 10). The only way his readers could recognise such teaching would be if they already had a clear grasp and firm commitment to what the Bible actually teaches.

It is not without significance that the grand-scale disintegration of many major denominations in the Western world at this time has followed the systematic erosion of their doctrine of the Person and Work of Christ. Those same churches are now imploding over issues of human sexuality. John's climactic statement spells out how much is at stake 'Whoever abides in the teaching has both the Father and the Son' (2 John 9)—and thus, salvation itself.

The urgency of John's message, not just for the church of his own day, but the church through the ages, could hardly be clearer. If churches are to be places that are truly safe for those seeking a spiritual home, then they must also be sound in what they teach from Scripture.

21

Extraordinary Means of Grace

THE idea of 'the means of grace' has undergone an encouraging rehabilitation in the life and ministry of many Reformed churches in recent years. This has come as a healthy corrective to pressure from the wider church to embrace ideas and practices that seem more effective vehicles for church growth. However 'effective' these alternative means may have seemed, it has been at the expense of a meaningfully biblical definition of the church. So, the widespread return to emphasising the Scriptures, sacraments, fellowship, and prayer (Acts 2:42) as the core components of a faithful and effective church has been welcome. These 'ordinary' means of grace are God's ways of communicating his great salvation in Christ by his Holy Spirit. The very fact, however, that the adjective 'ordinary' is applied to these means by which God works implies that they are not the only way he works. They may be normative, but they are not exhaustive.

The Westminster Assembly elaborated on how the ordinary means are used by God in their treatment of Effectual Calling in chapter 10 of the *Westminster Confession of Faith*. It deals with the means by which the call of the gospel (which is universal) is made to be effective in the lives of 'All those whom God hath predestinated unto life' (WCF 10.1).

The divines open up what this entails and how it happens as being, 'at his appointed and accepted time' and by means of 'his Word [i.e. the Scriptures] and Spirit' in order that they may be actually lifted 'out of that state of sin and death, in which they are by nature, to grace and salvation, by Jesus Christ; enlightening their minds spiritually and savingly to understand the things of God, taking away their heart of stone, and giving unto them an heart of flesh; renewing their wills, and, by His almighty power, determining them to that which is good, and effectually drawing them to Jesus Christ: yet so, as they come most freely, being made willing by His grace' (WCF 10.1).

They go on in the next section to explain this further: 'This effectual call is of God's free and special grace alone, not from anything at all foreseen in man, who is altogether passive therein, until, being quickened and renewed by the Holy Spirit, he is thereby enabled to answer this call, and to embrace the grace offered and conveyed in it' (WCF 10.2).

Here, then, are the normal means God uses to bring the spiritually dead to life, enabling them to turn in repentance and faith towards God as they rest on Christ alone for their salvation. But they are not the only means. The very next section goes on to make this clear in what it says about 'elect infants dying in infancy': 'Elect infants, dying in infancy, are regenerated, and saved by Christ, through the Spirit, who works when, and where, and how He pleases: so also are all other elect persons who are incapable of being outwardly called by the ministry of the Word [referring primarily to the preaching of the Scriptures]' (WCF 10.3). Thus, the confession acknowledges that there are certain circumstances of life in which the 'ordinary means of grace' cannot function.

The Westminster divines reiterate this point in chapter 14, 'Of Saving Faith.' There they state, 'The grace of faith, whereby the elect are enabled to believe to the saving of their souls, is the work of the Spirit of Christ in their hearts, *and is ordinarily wrought* by the ministry of the Word, by which also, and by the administration of the sacraments, and prayer, it is increased and strengthened' (WCF 14.1) [italics added].

There are at least two reasons for drawing attention to the fact God's grace has extraordinary as well as ordinary dimensions.

The first is pastoral. Infant mortality may not be as common in developed countries in the twenty-first century as it was in those same countries just a few centuries ago, but the pain of loss and questions about life and destiny it raises are just as real. In some respects, they are even more real for Christian parents who believe that 'faith comes from hearing, and hearing through the word of Christ' (Rom. 10:17). Knowing something of God's extraordinary grace for such extraordinary circumstances can only bring comfort.

The fact the scope of this principle goes beyond 'elect infants dying in infancy' to 'all other elect persons who are incapable of being outwardly called by the ministry of the Word' is also pastorally significant. Not least in terms of how the church regards and cares for those who are mentally incapacitated. At a very basic level the questions must be asked, 'Can they be accepted as members of the church?' and 'May they receive the Lord's Supper?' If a church turns 'the ordinary means of grace' into 'the sole means of grace,' the answer must be 'No.'

The other reason for raising this issue relates to the question Jesus was asked *en route* to Jerusalem: 'Lord, will those who are saved be few?' (Luke 13:23). It is the question many have asked throughout the centuries. And it is significant that Jesus does not give a direct answer. Rather, he says the real issue is making sure we, ourselves, are in his kingdom (Luke 13:24).

This does not mean the question in itself is wrong, or that it is wrong to ask it. Interestingly it was taken up by several nineteenth century Reformed theologians, among them, W. G. T. Shedd and Charles Hodge, in their consideration of the so-called 'Larger Hope.'

In his book, *Calvinism: Pure and Mixed—A Defence of the Westminster Standards*, Shedd deals with this question in a chapter entitled 'The "Larger Hope."'[3] There he discusses this issue in light of the relation between God's glory and the number of the redeemed, but with cognizance of the extra-ordinary dimensions in the operations of grace.

Charles Hodge also addresses the issue in his comments on Romans 5:18-20, where he says,

---

[3] W. G .T. Shedd, *Calvinism: Pure and Mixed* 1893; repr. (Edinburgh: Banner of Truth Trust, 1986) pp. 92-131.

We have no right to put any limit on these general terms, except what the Bible itself places upon them… All the descendants of Adam, except Christ, are under condemnation; all the descendants of Adam, except those of whom it is expressly revealed that they cannot inherit the kingdom of God, are saved. This appears to be the clear meaning of the apostle, and therefore he does not hesitate to say that where sin abounded, grace has much more abounded, that the benefits of redemption exceed the evils of the fall; that the number of the saved far exceeds the number of the lost.[4]

This issue has had extensive coverage by Roman Catholic, Liberal Protestant and Evangelical Protestant authors from a range of differing perspectives and with correspondingly different conclusions. But all too frequently their concern has been to try to justify, at one end of the spectrum, 'sincere' faith in any religious context, or good works in all contexts as the basis of acceptance with God; or, at the other end, some form of universalism. It is significant, therefore, that the issue was raised in the way it was by the Reformed theologians cited above. But is even more significant to see the theological foundation on which they build their argument and from which they draw their conclusions. It rests entirely on the free grace and mercy of God—which are not limited by a person's age or mental capacity.

The questions are real but Scripture is noticeably silent on them. Nevertheless, the men of the Westminster Assembly

[4] Charles Hodge, *Systematic Theology,* vol. 1 (New York: Scribner & Co, 1872), p. 26.

offer a judicious response in what they say in relation to effectual calling. They enable us to focus on what the Bible makes clear—that the church's duty is to 'Go therefore and make disciples of all nations' (Matt. 28:19, 20)—while at the same time acknowledging that 'the Judge of all the earth' will most certainly do what is right (Gen. 18:25).

SECTION FOUR

LIVING THE PILGRIM LIFE

I therefore, a prisoner for the Lord, urge you to walk in a manner worthy of the calling to which you have been called, with all humility and gentleness, with patience, bearing with one another in love, eager to maintain the unity of the Spirit in the bond of peace. There is one body and one Spirit—just as you were called to the one hope that belongs to your call—one Lord, one faith, one baptism, one God and Father of all, who is over all and through all and in all. But grace was given to each one of us according to the measure of Christ's gift. Therefore it says,

'When he ascended on high he led a host of captives,
    and he gave gifts to men.'

(In saying, 'He ascended', what does it mean but that he had also descended into the lower regions, the earth? He who descended is the one who also ascended far above all the heavens, that he might fill all things.) And he gave the apostles, the prophets, the evangelists, the shepherds and teachers, to equip the saints for the work of ministry, for building up the body of Christ, until we all attain to the unity of the faith and of the knowledge of the Son of God, to mature manhood, to the measure of the stature of the fullness of Christ, so that we may no longer be children, tossed to and fro by the waves and carried about by every wind of doctrine, by human cunning, by craftiness in deceitful schemes. Rather, speaking the truth in love, we are to grow up in every way into him who is the head, into Christ, from whom the whole body, joined and held together by every joint with which it is equipped, when each part is working properly, makes the body grow so that it builds itself up in love.

Ephesians 4:1-16

22

The Fear of the Lord

GIVEN the frequency with which 'the fear of the LORD,' or one of its variants, is mentioned in the Bible, it is more than a little unusual that so little seems to be said about it in the church today. It is surely here that we must begin if we are to truly understand what it means to know him as our God and follow him as one of his pilgrim people.

In all too many cases a focus on the immanence and intimacy of God as revealed in Scripture has been given such precedence over his transcendence and majesty that the latter have been all but eclipsed. The effect of this is not merely to create an inadequate view of God, but also a deficient understanding of what it means to relate to him. The Bible does not allow us to do either.

The keynote sounded in the book of Proverbs is that 'the fear of the LORD is the beginning' of both 'knowledge' (1:7) and 'wisdom' (9:10). In other words, the key to a sound epistemology in life as well as to the requisite 'skill for living'—concepts bound together in the Hebrew words—is a right disposition towards God.

It would be nice to simply assume that the notion of what it means to 'fear' God is sufficiently understood in the Reformed and evangelical community that it does not need further definition or explanation. But I am not convinced this is the case for the present generation. The years during which this concept has been neglected or marginalised have meant that, for many, this is something of an unfamiliar, or perhaps even a worrying concept. Therefore, a brief elucidation may be in order, not least because the vocabulary of fear in Scripture is nuanced by the context in which it appears.

Perhaps the best example of this is seen in what happened immediately after God gave Israel the Ten Commandments at Mt. Sinai (Exod. 20:18-21). The Israelites saw thunder and lightning and heard the sound of the trumpet (Exod. 20:18, 19). They were witnessing a theophany, an observable appearance of God, and it had a profound effect on them. They 'were afraid and trembled' and 'stood far off' and they pleaded with Moses to act as a mediator between them and God (Exod. 20:18, 19).

Their reaction is in many ways understandable, but what is both interesting and instructive is how Moses responded to them. He said, 'Do not fear, for God has come to test you, that the fear of him may be before you, that you may not sin' (Exod. 20:20). At first glance his statement seems to be a contradiction in terms. On the one hand, he told them not to be afraid and on the other, he said that God's purpose in this was to teach them to fear. So clearly Moses had in mind two very different kinds of fear that are possible for God's believing people.

One is what an older generation of theologians sometimes called 'craven fear,' that is, a holy dread of God because of his nature and attributes. There is, without question, a place for that. God should indeed fill us with dread, in part because of his otherness as our eternal creator, but also because of his character as the holy, just, and righteous one. The writer to the Hebrews captures this well when he says, 'our God is a consuming fire' (Heb. 12:29) and 'it is a fearful thing to fall into the hands of the living God' (Heb. 10:31). Regardless of the blessings of his immanence, the sheer transcendence of God is awesome in the ultimate sense of that word.

It is only when we grasp the fear that is associated with the otherness of God that we can truly begin to appreciate the kind of fear that Moses had in view in what he said to Israel. He told them that there was something quite deliberate in the way that God had revealed himself to them on that occasion. God showed them that they certainly did have good reason to be afraid of him. This was not only because he is the great law-giver, but because he is also the eternal law-enforcer and judge before whom every human being will one day stand. However, he is still more than that. He is none other than their Saviour-God, a fact he had reminded them of in the preface to the Ten Commandments, 'I am the LORD your God who brought you out of the land of Egypt, out of the house of slavery' (Exod. 20:2).

The fact that this detail precedes the giving of the Law has huge implications for the way it should be understood. At one level it cradles the terror of the Law in the comfort of the gospel for all who have come to know the Lord as their Saviour-God. Whereas the perfection and the penetrating power of the Ten Commandments exposes us all as lawbreakers, deserving its full penalty, it reminds us that our redemption comes from the very same God who has given it. In that sense the kind of 'fear' it is designed to generate in the hearts of those who know him in this way is (again to borrow the language of an older generation) 'filial fear': the respect sons and daughters show (or ought to show) to their parents.

Knowing God as the one who has delivered us (through his Son) from 'the futile ways' that once were ours (1 Pet. 1:18) and from a life of 'lawlessness' (1 John 3:4), serves only to intensify our highest regard for him as both just and gracious. It will lead us to love and serve him, not out of a sense of servile obligation; but in joyful devotion as his justified and adopted children in Christ.

Going back to Moses' explanation to the Israelites at Sinai, the fear or reverence God was seeking to instil in them through this encounter was 'that [they] may not sin.' That is, it was intended to encourage their obedience. In that light, we cannot help but see how much the church, as the New Israel, needs to learn that lesson all over again. A rediscovery of what it means to fear the Lord will impact the kind of worship we offer (Heb. 12:28), the service we render (2 Cor. 7:1) and the witness we bear to a hostile world (1 Pet. 3:15). Therein lies the foundation for knowledge and skill for living that will transform our lives and reach the world with the gospel.

23

Proof of Life

THE First Letter of John is an enigmatic, but hugely significant, part of the Bible. At first glance its message seems very straightforward, but on closer inspection it is incredibly complex (as I discovered to my chagrin when I started preaching 1 John). By John's own assertion, the biggest idea he is addressing is how a person can know they have 'eternal life' (1 John 5:13). It ties in with his stated reason for writing the Gospel that bears his name: 'these [things] are written so that you may believe that Jesus is the Christ, the Son of God, and that by believing you may have life in his name' (John 20:31). He wrote the Gospel to tell people how to find this 'life-of-the-world-to-come,' and he wrote his first letter so they could be sure it is the genuine 'life-of-the-world-to-come' they have found.

The verses leading up to this statement help to bring it into focus in terms of where this certainty is located. They do so, not primarily from the perspective of personal assurance—'Have I really believed?'—but in the sense of 'What kind of gospel have I believed?' The two questions are not unrelated, but it is the latter which was the more pressing for the churches to which this circular letter was sent.

John was addressing a crisis situation that had arisen among churches under his oversight, probably in and around Ephesus. False teachers—whom he describes as 'antichrists' (1 John 2:18, 19)—had caused a major division within these congregations and caused significant turmoil and confusion. Although John does not explicitly tell us all the details of their teaching, he does give enough clues (as many commentators recognize) to suggest it was an early form of Gnosticism. It set up a false dichotomy between spirit and flesh that, in turn, led to a distorted view of morality. Since they regarded the spirit as the only thing that mattered, whatever they did 'in the flesh'—regardless how wicked—they considered to be of no consequence.

However, the most insidious element in this new teaching was its denial of the incarnation as taught by the apostles. That is, they did not regard Jesus as 'the Son of God come in the flesh.' Instead, they saw him as having either been 'adopted' in some sense as 'Son of God' temporarily (Adoptionism), or else as only seeming to have taken on a human nature, but one that was not real (Docetism). The heart of the apostolic gospel was being challenged, and the church was plunged into uncertainty and confusion over the nature of the 'eternal life' promised in the gospel. Thus, John sets out to clarify what that life is and how a person can be sure they have received it.

The apostle's argument reaches its climax at the beginning of the fifth chapter where he addresses the 'proof of life' question. Just as doctors speak about the 'vital signs' that demonstrate a person is alive and not dead—pulse, temperature, heart rate and blood pressure—so John points to the vital signs of its spiritual equivalent. He introduces them in a way that shows their interconnectedness (1 John 5:1, 2), showing that no one strand of proof in itself is sufficient to demonstrate this really is life from above, but only as it exists in relation to two others.

In that sense John is pointing not just to 'vital signs' of new life, but also to what scientists in a different context describe as the 'irreducible complexity' of life. Life exists, not when its component parts happen to be in the same place, but when they coexist in the same organism. So with the spiritual life that is constituted through regeneration. John argues that the coexistence of faith, love, and obedience in a person's life individually, and the shared life of the church to which they belong are both proof of life and confirmation of the gospel they have believed.

John builds an empirical argument to make his case. He argues for a faith that affirms 'Jesus is the Christ.' This faith expresses itself in love for God and for his people and does so consciously, as an act of obedience to God's commands (1 John 5:1, 2). Indeed, echoing the sum of the moral law as being love for God and for our fellow human beings, he points to obedience as the supreme expression of love, and argues (contra the false teachers) that God's commands are anything but onerous (1 John 5:3). This leads him to state unequivocally that faith in Jesus as the Son of God incarnate is the *only* means by which we can secure victory over the world (1 John 5:4, 5).

John presses home his argument concerning the apostolic Christ with an appeal to the threefold witness of 'the water,' 'the blood,' and 'the Spirit' (1 John 5:6-12). Appealing to the Old Testament requirement for two or three witnesses to validate a point in law (Deut. 19:15), he makes it clear that the Holy Spirit has provided that validation. The Spirit has done this in regard to the incarnate deity of Jesus Christ through his testimony at Jesus' baptism (Matt. 3:16, 17) and through the saving efficacy of his death—affirmed by his resurrection (Rom. 1:4). So, when someone trusts in Jesus as the 'Son of God,' the Holy Spirit affirms their faith within them (1 John 5:9, 10).

John leaves his readers in no doubt as to the vital significance of the Spirit's testimony to this core gospel truth. 'And this is the testimony, that God gave us eternal life, and this life is in his Son. Whoever has the Son has life; whoever does not have the Son of God does not have life' (1 John 5:11, 12). Assurance of salvation can never be divorced from the assured testimony of the apostolic gospel. The vital signs of real spiritual life go far beyond how we may feel about our faith to the Christ who is offered to us in the gospel, in whom we place our trust.[1]

---

[1] The *Westminster Shorter Catechism* answers question 86, 'What is faith in Jesus Christ?' with 'Faith in Jesus Christ is a saving grace, whereby we receive and rest upon him alone for salvation, *as he is offered to us in the gospel* [emphasis added].'

24

An Overview of Grace

'GRACE' could easily be seen as one of those doctrines every child from a Christian home ought to know from Kindergarten. Whether it be through the acronym *God's Riches at Christ's Expense*, or just the plain and often repeated 'God's unmerited favour,' it would be easy to check it off as 'learnt' and just move on. However, if we feel that way, then we should think again. Like many of the words that underpin and define great biblical truths, the apparent simplicity of 'grace' belies its depth and richness. This guided tour of the key facets of this doctrine that lies at the heart of the gospel is not merely meant to open up new horizons for those who have not gone much further than the above, but also as a refreshing reminder to others who have.

Grace as the de-merited favour of God (favour despite our actions which are deserving of censure) is undoubtedly the best place to start as we explore the dimensions of what it entails. Just as a person can only truly begin to grasp what 'love' is when they have been loved, so too with grace. To try and understand it merely through clinical etymology and definition, will fall far short of appreciating it in the full depth and wonder of what it means. It is hardly surprising that 'Amazing Grace,' the most popular hymn in the history of Christian hymnody, was penned by a man (an ex-slave trader) who knew it from the receiving end.

The most obvious use of this sense of 'grace' is in Ephesians where Paul captures the sheer wonder of redemption with the words, 'by grace you have been saved' (Eph. 2:5, 8). Having set what we are and deserve by nature over against what we become in Christ, 'grace' is salvation's only possible explanation. The favour God bestows in it does not merely lift us out of the depths, but up to the highest heights, to restored fellowship with him. Paul knew that in his own experience and he never tired of declaring it to be true for every Christian.

Grace also empowers us as God's children. It follows, from what the apostle says about the extreme nature of grace as the only antidote to the human condition, that when a person experiences this grace, it must make a visible impact on their life. The new life we have in Christ becomes visible in the new life we live for him. What we were powerless to do prior to our salvation we are empowered to do through our new-found life in the saviour. That is why Paul emphasises the fact salvation is 'not a result of works' (Eph. 2:9); but instead, we are 'created in Christ Jesus for good works' (Eph. 2:10). The very same grace through which we receive God's saving favour empowers us in Christ to do what would otherwise have been impossible.

Two chapters later in Ephesians we encounter the grace word again, this time used with another sense. Speaking to those who belong to the church, the body of Christ, he says, 'But grace was given to each one of us according to the measure of Christ's gift' (Eph. 4:7). Given what the apostle said earlier in the letter, this inevitably raises a question over what he means here. Is he suggesting that grace is experienced by degrees? If that were so, it would contradict what he has said already.

John Stott addresses this apparent anomaly in his commentary on Ephesians. He points to the context of this passage which relates to gifts and service in the life of the church, the people God calls into leadership and the goal of their ministry among his people (Eph. 4:11-13). Stott helpfully points out that the aspect of grace in view here is 'serving grace.' This aspect refers to particular gifts God gives to particular individuals. The Holy Spirit enables us to use the particular gifts he gives, and such gifts and enabling are not given uniformly to every Christian. Paul's point is simple: every member of the church must recognise their gifting and play their part so that the body may be built up (Eph. 4:14-16).

One of the great mistakes we often make in trying to establish a theology of grace is to construe it in a way that encourages passivity on our part as its recipients. Although that is true in a person's initial experience of grace, as seen under the first heading, it is not true in the outworking of grace in the Christian life. This is clearly implied in what we have just seen in relation to gifts and service where Paul issues an unmistakable call to action, but it comes out even more strikingly in what Paul says to Titus.

Having issued a series of exhortations to older and younger men and women and to slaves of both sexes, Paul says:

> For the grace of God has appeared, bringing salvation for all people, training us to renounce ungodliness and worldly passions, and to live self-controlled, upright, and godly lives in the present age, waiting for our blessed hope, the appearing of the glory of our great God and Saviour Jesus Christ... (Titus 2:11-13).

As we see in this passage, God's grace trains us. Through his word and by his example, our Lord instructs us in a way that rightly calls for our response.

Paul is not the only apostle to speak of grace. Peter frequently refers to it. He does so in all the senses already mentioned in relation to Paul, but he adds other nuances as well—for example, in how we use the gifts God gives his people (1 Pet. 4:10), or in a broader sense, the fulness of the favour and strength God freely gives his people (1 Pet. 5:5). Notably, however, he speaks of what John Piper describes as 'future grace' when he says, 'set your hope fully on the grace that will be brought to you at the revelation of Jesus Christ' (1 Pet. 1:13). He also refers to 'grace' as Christian character into which we must continually grow: 'But grow in the grace and knowledge of our Lord and Savior Jesus Christ' (2 Pet. 3:18). In other words, the grace that so fully characterises the Lord himself is the template of the kind of grace-filled character by which his people will be universally recognised. That leads into the final thought on this little tour.

As Sinclair Ferguson has pointed out in numerous places, there is a real temptation for Christians to turn 'grace' into a commodity: something to be dispensed by God, or accessed by his people when they are running on empty. But to do so is to miss the greatest thing of all about it. 'Grace' in its most glorious sense is embodied in the incarnate Christ.

None of the benefits of grace—those mentioned above or those mentioned elsewhere in Scripture—can be ours apart from Christ. If we do not have him, we can neither know nor experience any of the graces bound up with him. That is why Jesus could tell Nicodemus—who had spent so much of his life steeped in the Bible, earnestly pursuing holiness—he could not even 'see,' let alone 'enter,' God's kingdom if he had not been 'born from above.' To know Christ, therefore, is to experience and enjoy God's grace in all its fullness.

That is why someone once added the following words as a concluding verse to John Newton's famous hymn 'Amazing Grace':

> When we've been there ten thousand years,
>   Bright shining as the sun,
> We've no less days to sing God's praise
>   Than when we first begun.

25

Faith on the Edge of Reason

IN its definition of 'Saving Faith' the *Westminster Confession of Faith* enters a very significant caveat that is all too often overlooked. Namely, 'This faith is different in degrees, weak or strong; may be often and many ways assailed, and weakened, but gets the victory: growing up in many to the attainment of a full assurance, through Christ, who is both the author and finisher of our faith' (WCF 14.3). Its inclusion is important, not just as a statement of theological fact, but in terms of its pastoral relevance to many true believers whose faith is in crisis.

The extent of this problem in church life is not easy to gauge, because Christians who wrestle with doubt are often reluctant to admit to it for a variety of reasons. Indeed, this is true for all Christians; pastors are no less prone to it—their interest in this matter can unfortunately have professional as well as personal implications. The reality is the problem of doubt is present in the church to a far greater degree than we might imagine. It is rather like the proverbial iceberg: its visible tip may seem small and somewhat innocuous to the untrained eye, but 90% of the problem is hidden beneath the surface.

Thankfully the Scriptures are neither unaware of this problem, nor do they show embarrassment in acknowledging it publicly. We see it in some high-profile cases, like the prophet Jeremiah (Jer. 20:7-18) and John the Baptist (Luke 7:18-23). It constitutes an underlying theme in the General Epistles of Hebrews through Jude. However, we see it addressed most directly in the psalms, notably in Psalm 73. There the author speaks with such openness about this issue that it is clear his faith at this particular point in his experience found itself on the edge of reason.

The authorship of this psalm is attributed to Asaph, one of the Levites appointed by David as one of the official music directors for tabernacle worship (1 Chron. 15:16, 17). He would have been very much in the public eye amidst the worshipping community of Israel. For him to waver in his beliefs had serious potential to affect the faith of others. Yet, far from airbrushing such a spiritual crisis out of the biblical record, it is set forth with brutal honesty, demonstrating clearly that doubt does not automatically spell the end of faith.

The psalm begins with a great affirmation of faith: 'Truly God is good to Israel, to those who are pure in heart' (Psa. 73:1). It has the kind of liturgical ring to it that would suggest it was a refrain, a key component of Jewish worship. It affirmed God's covenant goodness and faithfulness. But juxtaposed to this great affirmation is Asaph's jarring confession that his faith was faltering. 'But as for me, my feet had almost stumbled, my steps had nearly slipped. For I was envious of the arrogant when I saw the prosperity of the wicked' (Psa. 73:2, 3).

Despite the comfort intended for the faithful as they rehearsed the great truths about God in worship, for Asaph it felt as though there was a yawning chasm between truth confessed and the apparent truth of the world in which he lived. He goes on to spell out where he saw these seeming incongruities. He catalogues the perceived blessings enjoyed by the wicked, over against the troubles he and the rest of the righteous were plagued by all day long (Psa. 73:4-14). Indeed, from the perspective of God's covenant to which he alludes in the opening verse, it seemed as though the blessings promised to the covenant faithful and the curses reserved for covenant-breakers in Deuteronomy 28–29 had somehow been reversed.

It has never been hard for Christians through the ages to identify with Asaph's words. It really does appear—at least as far as tangible, material blessings are concerned—as though those who openly deny God are more likely to 'prosper' by this world's standards, while those who are Christians and seek to live by the Bible's ethical standards and with integrity seem to be the losers. The issue has become even starker in recent years with the rise of militant atheism and the race between Western countries to embrace an anti-Christian ethic. Where is God and his promise to be good to the righteous in such times?

Asaph begins to answer that question even before he has finished laying out his complaint. On the one hand, he admitted that even to speak in the way he was speaking was a betrayal of the people who mattered far more to him than he had perhaps appreciated (Psa. 73:15). More than that, he confessed that there was more going on in this scenario than he was capable of comprehending (Psa. 73:16). (Which would suggest he knew there is an unseen dimension to life that changes how we understand the merely tangible.) This is how it should be for us, before we allow ourselves to be dragged too far down the road of doubt—fashionable or otherwise—we would do well to remember the limits of our own understanding as well as the testimony of other believers around us.

There is a critical turning point in the psalmist's journey to the edge of darkness. It is when he says, 'until I went into the sanctuary of God...' (Psa. 73:17). It is the point at which he gains a different perspective which changes everything.

In all of this, and in light of the Bible's candour as it speaks about this issue, we should appreciate more fully why the men of the Westminster Assembly chose to include their caveat about the nature of faith in the Confession. They were biblical realists and knew that faith leads us to salvation, not because it is perfect, but because it leads us to Christ. Sometimes it means, as it did for Asaph in the first half of Psalm 73, clinging to him as if just by our fingernails.

Section Five

Rejoicing in Hope and Heading for Home

Rejoice in the Lord always; again I will say, Rejoice. Let your reasonableness be known to everyone. The Lord is at hand; do not be anxious about anything, but in everything by prayer and supplication with thanksgiving let your requests be made known to God. And the peace of God, which surpasses all understanding, will guard your hearts and your minds in Christ Jesus.

Philippians 4:4-7

26

The Joy of God's Salvation

IN the American Declaration of Independence, 'the pursuit of happiness' was listed along with 'Life' and 'Liberty' as one of three 'inalienable rights' common to all people. It is a striking and curious inclusion. But whatever lay behind its place in this history-making document, it recognises that joy lies at the very heart of our humanity.

Around 130 years earlier another distinguished group, the men of the Westminster Assembly, enshrined joy in a very different document: the *Westminster Shorter Catechism*. In answering the first question, 'What is man's chief end?' they not only stated, 'Man's chief end is to glorify God,' but added, 'and to enjoy him forever.' This too, in the deepest possible way, acknowledges that to be joyful is of the essence of what it means to be human.[1]

The Westminster divines were recognising the fact that joy is woven deep into the tapestry of God's revelation in

---

[1] End (function or purpose) and essence (what we are) are interrelated. Humanity was designed both to reflect God's glory and to bring him glory through worship—both of which are bound up with joy of the highest order.

Scripture. From the pristine joy of Eden to the incomparably greater joy of heaven, it can be traced—even in the worst of times—through the history of redemption. It is strange, then, that joy so often seems to be missing from Christian experience and, more so, from worship. Even where Christians do seek to incorporate it into their life and worship, it often feels synthetic and comes across as a cheap imitation of the deep, enduring joy in the Bible.

This theme could hardly be more relevant to the world we live in. The American dream of 'happiness' seems further away than ever. The world at large appears to be sliding ever more deeply into a joyless existence. Yet the yearning for joy lives on, no matter how unattainable it may seem. So, in terms of gospel opportunity, for those who, in Adam, have been subjected to a life of toil and misery, Christ's declaration, 'I came that they may have life and have it abundantly' (John 10:10) should be shouted loud and clear. But for that to happen, those who supposedly have this new life should display it in their own lives in order to commend it to others.

All of this gives good reason to explore the theme of joy in Scripture more seriously than perhaps we do. Indeed, nowhere should this be more so than in churches that claim to be 'Reformed.' The *Westminster Shorter Catechism* was not compiled by men who treated doctrine lightly, yet they chose to embed joy in the very first line of the summary of all they believed. Thus, all who claim this heritage should be marked by joy in all its rich dimensions.

In speaking of this joy, we need to note a key marker the Bible itself lays down to understand the joy of which it speaks. However noble the ideal of 'happiness' in the Declaration of Independence may have been, it is undefined. So, almost universally, those who have pursued it have sought a version of happiness that is a merely human construct. People see wealth, success, sex and more besides as the key to pleasure, only to be painfully disappointed when they actually get what they want. The joy presented in the Bible is something very different.

Interestingly, this comes out most clearly in words penned by King David when he had all but lost this precious commodity. Ironically, it was at a time when he had pursued pleasure in the wrong way. Instead of finding deeper satisfaction, he allowed the joy he already had to slip through his fingers. In a moment of unrestrained lust, he thought that sex with Bathsheba would take his enjoyment of life to new levels, but it had the opposite effect. It sank him into the lowest depths of misery he had ever known. So, in his prayer of repentance and plea to God for help he cries out, 'Restore to me the joy of your salvation' (Psa. 51:12). It is the combination of 'joy' bound up with 'salvation' that is 'your' [God's] gracious gift that defines the uniqueness of the joy found in the gospel.

What we need is not 'joy' in some vague sense, or even a 'joy' that comes from 'salvation' in the multitude of ways this has been construed. Rather, the joy we need, and the only joy that truly satisfies the human spirit, is that which God alone can give through his gracious salvation. In his salvation, God deals with the one thing that has plunged our race into misery—our sin, its guilt and its consequences—through the atonement he provides. Not only this, he simultaneously restores the joy that was lost to our race in Adam's first sin: the joy of communion with God. The heart of God's salvation is the reconciliation of God to sinners and sinners to God.

David knew the joy of communion with God, but tried to improve on it through his union with Bathsheba. However, the misery he brought on himself was more painful than he could ever imagine—hence his longing to be restored. He discovered the hard way that there is nothing in the entire universe that can compare to the joy of God's salvation. We will explore this joy more fully in the remaining chapters. The joy this world needs and unwittingly longs for is the joy that only God can give us through his Son, our saviour Jesus Christ.

27

City of Joy

THE theme of joy in Scripture finds its focus in the joy of knowing God as our God and saviour. As we seek his glory (as opposed to our own) we experience a joy that is utterly different from all the joys of earth combined. Nevertheless, and amazingly, this joy can be found and experienced on earth.

The Israelites knew all about this. In fact, they wove it into their anthology of worship in the Book of Psalms in words that have been used by God's people down through the ages. Anticipating the joy of going up to meet with God in Jerusalem, the pilgrims would sing, 'I was glad when they said to me, "Let us go to the house of the LORD"' (Psa. 122:1). This psalm belongs to the group of psalms known as the 'Songs of Ascent' or 'pilgrim psalms.' These were psalms God's people would sing as they travelled to Jerusalem for the great feasts and festivals of the Old Testament calendar. They were community psalms. They expressed the sentiments of shared experiences of life generally, but this was within the shared experience of

God's great salvation. In this third 'pilgrim psalm' the singers express the joy bound up uniquely with meeting with God in his city.

Even though they knew the 'joys of life' each day in their homes and with the communities from which they came, the joy located in the city of God had a quality all of its own. But what did that mean? Clearly it was not merely the thrill of a tourist seeing the city of Jerusalem for the first time, or even returning to it for another year. There was much more to it, and the wording of the psalm helps us understand what this entailed.

At the most basic level it was the fact that Jerusalem was God's city. Even though it was recognised to be the city of David, the capital he established for Israel, it was far more. The fact that in the lyric of the second verse of the psalm, the singers address the city as if it were a person, 'O Jerusalem,' signals that this is no ordinary city. This detail picks up on many other references in the psalms and elsewhere in Scripture that identify the city in relation to God and not just to Israel or its kings.

Often Jerusalem is identified as 'Zion'—a name it already had prior to its first being captured by David from the Jebusites (2 Sam. 5:7). It was later used to refer to the city itself, sometimes more specifically to the Temple area, but also to the city as an earthly symbol of the eternal city of God. However, the Sons of Korah, in a psalm about the security of God's people, speak of it as 'the city of God, the holy habitation of the Most High. God is in the midst of her' (Psa. 46:4, 5). The one thing that set this city apart and made it a joyful refuge was the fact that it symbolised God's earthly dwelling with the temple as its epicentre.

The Jerusalem temple is in ruins, but the true temple still remains. Paul identifies the church as God's new temple in which he dwells by his Spirit (1 Cor. 3:16). This is not in the sense of a physical building, but, as Peter says, all those who have come to Christ as 'a living stone' through union with him become 'like living stones [who] are being built up as a spiritual house' (1 Pet. 2:4, 5). So the joy of Jewish believers as they went up to their beloved city is taken to a whole new level for Christian believers as they gather for worship as the church.

Psalm 122 develops this insight further in terms of the character of Jerusalem as being, 'built as a city that is bound firmly together' (Psa. 122:3). It is possible that this simply makes the observation, as any present day visitor to the Old Quarter of Jerusalem will know, that its streets were narrow and its houses tightly packed. But it could also be a vivid reference to its being a close-knit community. This seems to be echoed in the prayer for peace and prosperity that comes later in the psalm.

Why should this be a cause for rejoicing? Because its opposites—disunity and dysfunction, the hallmarks of a fallen race—are the cause of sorrow. Again, as we trace this through into New Testament teaching about the church, we appreciate why it emphasises not only the church as God's community, but especially the need to preserve its unity.

Once more, in the flow of the psalm, we are given a glimpse of how God safeguards the unity of his people.

It is by strong and stable government: 'There the thrones for judgment were set, the thrones of the house of David' (Psa. 122:5). Even though the throne of David was in the foreground, the psalm makes it clear there was also a higher throne in view. The pilgrims were to go up to Jerusalem, not to praise their current king, but 'the name of the Lord' (Psa. 122:4). So it is to the Lord, their eternal king, that they address their prayers (Psa. 122:6, 7).

The Lord and King of Israel is the same Lord and king who appeared in flesh and lived among us (John 1:14). He is the ultimate source of the peace (*shalom*) we need more than anything, and to him we joyfully come as we gather in his name each Lord's Day. We hear his word, we sing his praise, we enjoy the fellowship of his people, and we savour the sacraments of his love. The life of the church is enfolded under the righteous rule of its great king, the Son of David, Jesus—another reason for rejoicing.

The climax of this Old Testament psalm is actually found in the New Testament, in a letter addressed to Jews who had come to faith in Jesus as God's promised Messiah. To them (and to Christians of all ethnic backgrounds) the writer says, 'you have come to Mount Zion… the heavenly Jerusalem' (Heb. 12:22-24). The joy of faithful Jewish pilgrims, in the shadowlands of Old Testament times, is eclipsed by the inexpressible joy of those who live on this side of Calvary. We see clearly what they only saw dimly. In the light of New Testament teaching we realise that when the church gathers in the name of Christ, through the power of the Spirit it is the earthly high point of our communion with the triune

God and nothing less than a foretaste of heaven. So, as we set out on our 'pilgrimage' to church each Sunday, we should surely be singing, 'I was glad when they said to me, "Let us go unto the house of the LORD!"' We are heading for the City of Joy.

28

Joy that Seeks Us through Our Pain

THE French Jesuit priest and philosopher, Teilhard de Chardin (1881–1955) said, 'Joy is not the absence of pain.' Others have made the same observation repeatedly, either quoting de Chardin, or else expressing the same thought from their own perspective. It is hardly surprising that people are shocked by this claim. It jars with the prevailing notion that joy is found only in the good things of life. But, no matter how much we may try to fill our life with good things, we cannot exclude the bad, and ultimately, we cannot escape the dark shadow of death that casts its pall over life itself. It is, therefore, a vital truth about the joy we discover in the Bible and something we very much need to grasp if we are to experience this joy ourselves.

The Scottish minister, George Matheson, captured the richness of this distinctively biblical understanding of joy in the hymn, 'O love that wilt not let me go.' At first sight it may seem to focus on the theme of love; but, as the verses unfold, it homes in on the joy bound up with the love of God.

Matheson goes on to speak about a 'richer, fuller' life and a 'flickering torch' whose 'borrowed ray' is ultimately restored. But then comes what is arguably the most arresting verse of the entire hymn:

> O Joy that seekest me through pain,
>   I cannot close my heart to Thee;
> I trace the rainbow through the rain,
> And feel the promise is not vain
>   That morn shall tearless be.

The author gives the context for the hymn in his own words, explaining that it was 'written in the Manse of my former parish (Innellan, Argyleshire) one summer evening in 1882. It was composed with extreme rapidity; it seemed to me that its construction occupied only a few minutes, and I felt myself rather in the position of one who was being dictated to than of an original artist. I was suffering from extreme mental distress, and the hymn was the fruit of pain.'

As with all good hymns, this one was born, not out of a moment of inspired emotion, but out of rich and deep truths of Scripture. As we have noted in the previous chapters on joy, the Bible presents us with a joy that is not found naturally in this world. This joy is richer and deeper than the superficial alternatives people cling to, which only leave them feeling let down and empty.

We find many striking examples of this richer joy throughout the Bible. In Psalm 31, David was crying out to God in the midst of deep distress, yet he also declared, 'I will rejoice and be glad in your steadfast love.' At the end of his prophecy, at a time when Israel was facing major catastrophe, Habakkuk declared, 'Though the fig tree should not blossom, nor fruit be on the vines, the produce of the olive fail and the fields yield no food, the flock be cut off from the fold and there be no herd in the stalls, yet I will rejoice in the LORD; I will take joy in the God of my salvation' (Hab. 3:17, 18).

The most striking expression of this kind of joy is found in Romans, where Paul shows how the experience of deep joy is bound up with the great truths of the gospel. Having just explained how justification through faith, by grace is the basis of our new standing before God, he says, 'And we rejoice in the hope of the glory of God' (Rom. 5:2); but he goes on to say, 'More than that, we rejoice in our sufferings…' (Rom. 5:3). The unusual juxtaposition of these two dimensions of joy actually takes us to the very heart of the joy of our salvation. That is, the joy of being restored to God in Christ. This joy, bound up with the 'Love that wilt not let me go,' follows us to the darkest of places in our earthly experience.

The final stanza of Matheson's hymn enables us to grasp this more fully when it takes us to the darkest place of all: the cross of Christ. With poetic irony, in the midst of the kind of mental torment that caused the hymn writer to look inward and downward, the dark sufferings of Christ lifts his head to look, not merely at the anguish of his saviour, but to what those sufferings have secured for all who believe: 'life that shall endless be.'

Christian joy is more than just a perspective on life; it is the experience of that new life which is found only in Christ. The life that flows from being united with him: that is the key to our being reunited with God and knowing that we can never again be separated from him. So it is not without significance that Teilhard de Chardin's definition of joy was not just that it is 'not the absence of pain,' but is also 'the presence of God.' The 'joy that seeks us through our pain' is neither faceless, nor heartless; it is the joy of knowing the saviour God, whom to know is life eternal.

29

'For the Joy that Was Set before Him'

In Hebrews 12:2, the writer of Hebrews makes one of those 'stop-you-in-your-tracks' type statements that crops up in the Bible from time to time. He writes, 'who [i.e. Christ] for the joy that was set before him endured the cross, despising the shame, and is seated at the right hand of the throne of God' (Heb. 12:2). It is, of course, speaking of Christ and his sufferings on Calvary, but it is the strange inclusion of 'joy' in this statement that seems out of place.

There is a translation issue bound up with this verse that has a bearing on how it should be interpreted. It concerns the Greek word *anti* which can be taken either as 'for' or 'in place of.' In his commentary on Hebrews, Calvin prefers the latter option. He explains why: 'for he [the author] intimates, that though it was free to Christ to exempt himself from all trouble and to lead a happy life, abounding in all good things, he yet underwent a death that was bitter and in every way ignominious.'[2] William Lane, among others, adopts the same

---

[2] John Calvin, *Commentaries on the Epistle of Paul to the Hebrews*, vol. 22 (Grand Rapids, MI: Baker, 1979), pp. 312-313.

interpretation in his commentary.[3] The sense of the verse would then be that Christ relinquished the earthly joys that could rightly have been his and instead accepted the anguish of the cross in order to secure salvation for his people.

The majority of translations and commentaries, however, opt for the translation 'for,' with the sense that Jesus was looking beyond the cross to what it would achieve as the supreme incentive for enduring its pain and shame. (Calvin acknowledges the legitimacy of this interpretation, though adding, 'I still prefer the former exposition.') Regardless of which translation we might deem preferable, the weight of joy in this statement is set against the weight of suffering with the implication that the former far outweighs the latter.

This thought has already surfaced in the New Testament where Paul tells the Romans, 'For I consider that the sufferings of this present time are not worth comparing with the glory that is to be revealed to us' (Rom. 8:18). Suffering weighs heavily on us all—even as Christians—but the burden of suffering is nothing compared to the glory to be revealed. The value of the glory far exceeds it, and that glory is bound up with joy.

How then, did the statement in Hebrews about joy in relation to the sufferings of Christ help the Christians to whom it was first addressed? The answer lies in what it says about Christ's horizons in life. Throughout the letter, Jesus has been presented not just as the incarnate Son of God, but also as the example of a perfect human. He is human, being the one who 'had to be made like his brothers in

[3] W. L. Lane, *Hebrews 9–13*, WBC (Waco, TX: Word, 1991).

every respect' (Heb. 2:17), but is also perfect, being the one who, as our priestly representative, 'in every respect has been tempted as we are, yet without sin' (Heb. 4:15). In the language of Paul, he is the 'second man' and 'last [ultimate] Adam' (1 Cor. 15:45-48). He had to be such to undo the damage done through Adam's fall in Eden, but it was also necessary so that he might become the model human. He is the paradigm for the new life that begins in salvation.

Clearly for these Hebrew Christians, the attraction of this world's pleasures (partial and polluted though they are) was undermining their determination to press on in the life of faith, and that was costing them so dearly. Hence the note the author strikes repeatedly in his catalogue of faithful saints from Old Testament times and their willingness to be true to God and accept suffering rather than betray him for a moment of pleasure. Moses is held up as the classic example of what this means: 'choosing rather to be mistreated with the people of God than to enjoy the fleeting pleasures of sin. He considered the reproach of Christ greater wealth than the treasures of Egypt, for he was looking to the reward' (Heb. 11:25, 26).

If there is any statement that helps us exegete (draw out) the enigmatic reference to Christ's attitude to suffering and joy in the twelfth chapter, this statement about Moses is it. As the one to whom Moses ultimately pointed, Jesus chose to deliberately eschew the pleasures of this world for the perfect joys and pleasure of the coming world. He knew that the purpose behind his earthly mission was to plumb the depths of sorrow for his people in order that he might be their trailblazer to the heights of everlasting joy.

Through his sufferings on Calvary, Jesus provided the only true and safe horizon whereby his people can navigate their way through life. He gives balance and perspective on how we are to view life. Far from suggesting that joy has no place in Christian experience, or that we are to somehow enjoy our suffering, he reminds us of where our priorities must lie. Since what matters most is the joy bound up with God being truly glorified through the restoration of his good creation, we can joyfully endure sufferings in this present world for the sake of what is to come.

Easter is the perfect season to remind us of this great reality. The darkness and despair of Good Friday give way to the joy of Easter Sunday. The Christ who suffered, bled, and died for us—the man of sorrows, acquainted with grief (Isa. 53:3)—is the same Christ who is risen for us and who is alive for evermore. He is our great high priest, enthroned in the highest place of honour and authority, who 'always lives to make intercession' for his people (Heb. 7:25). His prayers will carry us through our sorrows and guarantee the fullness of joy he has prepared for us in heaven.

30

Fullness of Joy and Pleasures For Evermore

THE very first John Piper book I read was *Future Grace*. Its title is taken from Peter's exhortation, 'set your hope fully on the grace that will be brought to you at the revelation of Jesus Christ' (1 Pet. 1:13). It provides the important reminder that no matter how great our experience of grace may be in this present age, it will take on a whole new dimension in the age to come. This well sums up the thread of teaching we have been exploring in this final section under the title, *Rejoicing in Hope and Heading for Home*. However rich and deep our joys on earth may be, they are nothing compared to our future experience in heaven. As Paul says, 'What no eye has seen, nor ear heard, nor the heart of man imagined, what God has prepared for those who love him' (1 Cor. 2:9). This is vitally important to our hope as Christians—not merely for our comfort in salvation, but also for our witness to the world.

David expresses this truth in Psalm 16, a song he wrote possibly while on the run from Saul. His train of thought traces the joy of his salvation through to its ultimate destination in the world to come. The older King James Version captures it poetically: '…in thy presence is fullness of joy; at thy right hand there are pleasures for evermore' (Psa. 16:11).

However, to appreciate the full weight of what David means in Psalm 16, we need to set these words in their wider context. Then several things become clear about 'future grace' and the joy bound up with it.

The hope and joy God promises for the future is not unconnected to our new life as God's people in the present. This was true for David, but every child of God needs to remember it. Too many Christians have a 'hope' for the future that bears no resemblance to the present and therefore can seem ethereal and detached from reality. As we look more closely at what David says, we shall see that his words about hope for the future are grounded in his experience of God in the present.

He begins with a prayer: 'Preserve me, O God, for in you I take refuge' (Psa. 16:1). His declaration of trust underpins his request for safety. He spells this out further: 'You are my Lord; I have no good apart from you' and 'the saints' are 'the excellent ones, in whom is all [his] delight' (Psa. 16:2, 3). He goes on to reaffirm his confidence in God who has proved himself trustworthy in every circumstance as the God of covenant faithfulness (Psa. 16:5, 6). This spills over into a declaration of praise and commitment to God (Psa. 16:7, 8). But it is David's summation in the next verse that is so telling: 'Therefore my heart is glad, and my whole being rejoices; my flesh also dwells secure' (Psa. 16:9). His hope for the future was firmly rooted in the present. Indeed, this hope is not merely 'spiritual' rest; it is both real and physical. Our bodies are every bit as much a part of 'us' as are our spirits.

What David says next is startling because he lived in the Old Testament era: '…you will not abandon my soul to Sheol [i.e. the place of the dead, the grave], or let your holy one see corruption' (Psa. 16:10). This was extraordinary because what God had revealed about a future life at that time was extremely limited. There was no clear doctrine of resurrection at this stage redemptive history.

How, then, do we account for David's bold claim about the future of the body of God's 'holy one'? In part he is pointing to God's promised Messiah. Both Peter and Paul reach for this verse to explain how Jesus' resurrection lay at the very heart of God's purpose in redemption. It would be wrong, however, to see this verse merely as some sort of prophetic insertion. If that were the case, it would be out of step with the tenor of the psalm as a whole. (Not least because it loses sight of the connection between David as the anointed one who anticipated the ultimate anointed one whom God would one day send.)

So, at the very least, as David reached for these words, he was declaring his confidence that even death could not rob him of the joys and blessings of salvation. David could face the future—even beyond this world—because God had proved himself to be faithful in the present. This is precisely what the apostles would have us grasp more fully in the light of Christ's resurrection. The grave has been robbed of its victory; therefore, Christians can die in peace, knowing our future joy remains intact.

The climax of the psalm spells out the link between David's present experience and his future confidence. The eternal nature of the joy of salvation—in terms of quality as much as duration—is the fact that it is 'in [God's] presence' and 'at [God's] right hand' (Psa. 16:11). The Lord himself is the key to this joy. It is found in union and communion with him. David's words echo the Aaronic blessing where the joy of benediction is tied to the presence and favour of God. God graciously turns his face towards his people.

This joy, however, is a pale reflection of a greater reality: the joy within the godhead. We glimpse this in the prologue to John's Gospel where he says the Word (Greek: *Logos*) was 'with [towards] God' (John 1:1). The joy of the Trinity is in the perfect fellowship of the three persons, in mutual love and enjoyment. Adam and Eve were created to share that joy as God's creatures, but they lost it through the fall. How, then, can this joy be restored? David answers, 'You have made known to me the path of life.' The path that leads to the life of everlasting joy begins in this world: at the cross where Christ secured salvation and guaranteed future grace with all its joys through the blood of the everlasting covenant.

BANNER
of TRUTH

The Banner of Truth Trust originated in 1957 in London. The founders believed that much of the best literature of historic Christianity had been allowed to fall into oblivion and that, under God, its recovery could well lead not only to a strengthening of the church, but to true revival.

Interdenominational in vision, this publishing work is now international, and our lists include a number of contemporary authors, together with classics from the past. The translation of these books into many languages is encouraged.

A monthly magazine, *The Banner of Truth*, is also published, and further information about this, and all our other publications, may be found on our website, banneroftruth.org, or by contacting the offices below:

Head Office:
3 Murrayfield Road
Edinburgh
EH12 6EL
United Kingdom
Email: info@banneroftruth.co.uk

North America Office:
PO Box 621
Carlisle, PA 17013
United States of America
Email: info@banneroftruth.org